Cultivating Words

The Guide to Writing about the Plants and Gardens You Love

The complete guide to writing about plants and gardens for home gardeners, garden designers, landscape architects, green-industry professionals — anyone who wants to translate passion for plants and gardens into words

By Paula Panich

 TRYPHON PRESS
NORTHAMPTON, MASS.

Cultivating Words:
The Guide to Writing
about the Plants and
Gardens You Love

Design and illustrations © 2005 Lynn Zimmerman

Published by Tryphon Press

ISBN 0-9762709-0-0
Library of Congress Control Number: 2005904578

Book orders:
Nancy Quick
Publishers Storage & Shipping Corp.
46 Development Road, Fitchburg, MA 01420
phone: 978-829-2527; fax: 978-348-1233
E-mail: orders@pssc.com
Web site: www.cultivatingwords.com

Printed in Canada

For Bill Linsman and
Ilana Panich-Linsman,
my roots in this world
and
In loving memory of
Saveta Gerič Panič
(1901–1986)
and
Julka Gerič Smith
(1904–1993)

Contents

Acknowledgments

This book is largely the result of the goodwill and faith shown by many people, especially Sabine Stezenbach, of the New York Botanical Garden; Richard Wiesenthal, formerly of the Institute of Ecosystem Studies; and Elisabeth Cary, of the Berkshire Botanical Garden, who believed in the idea of teaching writing about plants and gardens.

Thank you to Jenny Silver and Ruah Donnelly, two passionate writer-gardeners who have helped shape this book; and to Helen Pratt, who blessed it early on.

Cultivating Words would not have been possible without the stimulating semester I spent in 2004 teaching at Boston University. My thanks to Susan Blau, who hired me (and by extension, to Charles Merzbacher), and to the students who kept the conversation going once the semester ended: Sara Hatch, Brittany Oat, Elizabeth McKee, Julia Fenwick, and Brendan Molloy.

My thanks to two excellent writers and teachers, Ron Carlson and Vivian Gornick.

Thank you to Elaine Greene for our conversation about the personal essay and the garden.

All books have early incubators. I would especially like to thank Mark Motta, who helped develop the title of this book, as well as the chapter titles; Steve Bergsman; and as always, Mark Greenside.

Thank you to my writing friends and colleagues who read chapters of this book in manuscript: Jenny Silver, Mark Adams, Christian McEwen, Maryann Macdonald, Trish Marx, Mark Greenside, Steve Bergsman, and Paul Morris. Many thanks to this book's general editor, John Bowman, whose optimism and excellent advice kept me writing and improving.

My gratitude to Mark Adams, Edite Cunhā, Susan Barker, Barbara Adler, Maryann Macdonald, Erica Browne Grivas, and Eugene Lawrence for their work as it appears in this book.

Thank you to the passionate gardener, fabulous cook, and wonderful designer and illustrator Lynn Zimmerman, who made this book her own.

There are no words to describe my debt and gratitude to Doris Troy, guiding muse. She was available at any hour of the day or night to discuss, cajole, wheedle, praise, phrase, or parse. She also copy edited and proofread this book. (May readers be blessed enough to hear these words someday: "When your book is in *my* house, it's *my* book too.")

And my gratitude to my very own professor, Bill Linsman, who held up the roof while I worked on this book and who listened as it was read aloud.

The Fragrance of Peaches:
Why I Wrote This Book

I wrote this book because of peaches. The fragrance of peaches, really. The image of "peach" comes to mind, and a sweet-ripe-fuzzy memory-fragrance intoxicates. This is not a sensory memory of a peach grower yearning for the summer harvest. I don't grow peaches; I can't imagine having a peach tree.

I wrote this book because I smell peaches in a classroom in the Bronx in the dead of winter, when students tiptoe in and take a seat at a sedan-sized table. They might whisper hello, or not. They are Broadway singers, floral arrangers, newspaper editors, physicians, stay-at-home parents, graduate students, nursery owners, kindergarten teachers — that is to say, adults. But they are anxious, tentative, worried — and all the while, I am smelling peaches, and smiling.

The classroom is in a building at the New York Botanical Garden. Besides anxiety and worry, what the students have in common is their absolute love for plants and gardens.

The root of their anxiety is this: They have come to a writing class. They know they are going to be asked to write something, perhaps for the first time since they left school, or at least for the first time in decades. They are terrified of judgment, making mistakes, and looking a fool.

They are forgetting about what else they bring to this Bronx classroom: love, passion, and the privilege of having spent years on their knees, their hands in dirt, bringing forth beauty into a world ever hungry for it.

I am smiling because in my years of teaching garden writing, I know these new students are ripe to write about what they love and know. That's where the peaches come in. The students are ready and eager to share their knowledge.

Gardeners are among the most generous people on earth. How often do you return from the house of a gardener thirsty, or empty-handed? Gardeners are often eager to "get down on the page" their hard-earned knowledge about plants, gardens, food, technique, or life.

Each generation of gardeners must be educated anew. If gardeners, and by gardeners I mean anyone who gardens for pleasure or by profession, feel the desire to communicate what they have learned, that's where this book comes in.

It is my job to break down the craft of nonfiction writing into discrete parts — to describe, for example, the news story or a profile. (Gardeners love writing profiles, a great form for picking the expert brain of, say, a renowned salvia grower, especially when the subject is valued by the interviewer.)

It's not the job of this book, however, to churn out professional garden journalists (although it might happen, as it sometimes does as a result of garden writing workshops), even if a book were able to do such a thing. It's my job to show how professional nonfiction garden writing is made and to encourage the practice of the craft, bit by bit. This is how writers, like gardeners, are made.

I wrote this book to be a practical guide for novice writer-gardeners and gardening writers. Even if you have never written before but have been requested "to write something" for your garden club or community newspaper on, perhaps, heirloom tomatoes — a subject you may know everything or nothing about — this book will help you.

Contributions of articles to the *New York Times* or book contracts are not expected. Yet you may publish work on beloved garden-related subjects in bulletins, community newsletters and newspapers, plant society publications, local gardening publications, on the Web. Well, you get the idea.

When you understand how writing is akin to gardening, you will lose much of your fear of the page, and your fear of judgment. In a workshop, other writer-gardeners will see a manuscript as a work in progress, just as they would a garden in early spring.

I wrote this book because of the pleasure I feel when former students publish something for the first time. Their pride is also mine.

I wrote this book in gratitude for what my students at the New York Botanical Garden and the Institute for Ecosystem Studies and elsewhere, from local horticultural societies to universities, have taught me about writing and gardening and life. In gardening, as in writing, skill serves readiness. Hand becomes the instrument of heart.

You already know that with gardening, one thing leads to another. One tricolor salvia will lead to a dozen; before you know it, every culinary salvia that can be grown in your USDA Zone ends up in an impeccably structured potagère. In the same way, poets may try reviewing movies; advertising copywriters write screenplays; reporters become novelists; garden writers become memoirists. It's the way of gardening, art, and life — letting a thousand flowers bloom.

I wrote this book in gratitude for the fragrance of peaches, and for the chance to say: *Gardening* and *writing* are synonyms for *love*.

Thoughts on How Writing Is Like Gardening

When we try to pick out anything by itself, we find it hitched to everything else in the universe. —John Muir

SAVETA AND JULKA GERIĆ were devoted sisters. They sewed, quilted, crocheted, and tatted. They roasted, stirred, baked, and canned. They stretched and smoothed satiny dough over long tables to cut noodles with precise hands. They also tilled, planted, watered, thinned, clipped, pruned, babied, and harvested.

They did all this, and more. Saveta, my grandmother, her long red hair caught in a crinkly white cap, toiled in a rubber factory for half a century. She retired, with a gold watch, when I was in first grade.

A quartet of hands shaping my childhood.

My grandmother and great-aunt were impeccable craftswomen. What they made was practiced, perfect. They weren't women who wanted sticky fingers on their works in progress: A child could look but not touch. They were focused, serious, intent on success at all costs. Tear out those stitches, toss that cake, restake those tomatoes. If things go awry, start over.

When I began to click away on my first computer, I had an image of my grandmother, her right foot pumping out an unerring rhythm on the treadle of her Singer.

GARDENING, COOKING, SEWING, knitting, quilting, art making, writing — whatever the effort — spring from the same sources. We are inexorably connected to and made up of the elements of our world, be they hydrogen, oxygen, nitrogen, sunlight, rain, tomatoes, wheat, flax, or cotton. Our human nature calls us to make things of our world and of ourselves. We combine and recombine the elements of our natural and spiritual world, using chemistry, physics, heart, mind, and hands. We work from necessity, from love, from desire, from our ideas of God or not-god, from hunger, from fear, from the urge to express what is within — from all of it.

One of the purposes of life is to learn to see. Gardeners and writers express what they see outside themselves and what they see within. When we practice time-consuming and heart-engaging activities, we learn to see. We make something of our world.

MOST GARDENERS CANNOT not garden. It's a double negation of the life force. We can't imagine not co-creating with the forces of nature to bring forth a personal vision from the ground we've been given to till. If we must move from our gardens, we plant anyway — in pots outside or on windowsills or in our imagination. We want and need to see the miracle of spring. We tuck in this hydrangea with that ivy, this ornamental grass with that evergreen. We want to see what will happen.

Many of us feel that way about words — what will happen when we combine them? Will the whole be greater than its parts?

Here are some thoughts from gardening writers:

> The girls (our two donkeys) love it when I weed the borders along the fence. I throw the weeds over and they have a treat. Some of these weeds grow on their side of the fence, but they taste better if I've pulled them up first; perhaps it is the presentation.
>
> I weed my stories, pulling out adjectives, clichés, tired language that slips into the first draft. I am imagining now throwing these

words and phrases over the fence to the girls: Here are some nasty superlatives. Yum.

In the garden and on the page I work with form. My garden has bones, as do my stories. Ideas germinate and unfurl like seeds. A seed was lodged into my mind today while I was with a friend. Later, driving along, it sprouted into a story. I have a title — "Undertow" — and I have a theme. It will take some time for it to break through the soil, reach for light, and unfold on the page.

—Edite Cunhã, novelist, short-story writer, artist, gardener

In writing and in the garden, you use implements. Dirt is involved. You bury things, you dig them up. You have to weed and prune; sometimes you sweat. You shovel a lot of shit . . . you can create a rose.

—Susan Barker, poet, artist, gardener

I muse. I walk around and muse some more. I write a few ideas, or sketch, in the case of the garden. I buy plants after more musing — or I write some more. I walk around. I place and unplace plants or words. I muse some more. I dig holes. I prune, prune, prune.

—Barbara Adler, poet, book artist, gardener

Gardening is largely a question of mixing one sort of plant with another sort of plant, and seeing how they marry happily together; if you see that they don't marry happily, then you must hoick one of them out and be quite ruthless about it. That is the only way to garden. The true gardener must be brutal, and imaginative for the future.

—Vita Sackville-West, genius of Sissinghurst, novelist, garden writer

WRITING, LIKE GARDENING, is an act of culture. In each, there are spaces to be cultivated not only with the hand and the body, but also with the spirit and the heart. No matter how lowly the gardening or writing task, the underlying passion for plants and gardens and writing justifies the effort. We love the interplay of nature and human labor, and love seeing our part in what is greater than ourselves. It's not easy to garden and it's not easy to write, but both can be accomplished with patience, practice, and the slow accretion of skill, nerve, and verve. The best of us — gardeners, writers, bakers, candlestick makers — grow bigger each time we are willing to tear down in order to build up again. To be *brutal, and imaginative for the future.*

CHAPTER ONE

What Is Garden Writing?

On this fine mid-August morning, blissfully cool, the seeds of my final crop of lettuces of the season safely tucked into a raised bed, two books with lush covers on my writing desk beg for attention. One is Richard Jaynes's *Kalmia: Mountain Laurel and Related Species;* the other is *Cultivating Delight: A Natural History of My Garden,* by Diane Ackerman.

Who are these garden writers? Richard Jaynes is a nursery owner (Broken Arrow Nursery in Hamden, Connecticut), plant geneticist, and horticulturist. He worked at the Connecticut Agriculture Experimental Station for close to a quarter of a century before becoming a nurseryman in 1984. He has been in love with kalmia for forty years. (*Kalmia latifolia* is a stunning evergreen flowering shrub native to North America. It's a member of the Heath family, along with rhododendrons, azaleas, blueberries, and cranberries.)

I have a mountain laurel, about sixty years old, near our front door. Nine feet tall, its curving, twisting architectural presence anchors this corner of the house in a way that its immediate neighbor, a rather dour, Calvinist-looking deutzia, cannot. Both bloom in spring, but even the flowers of the mountain laurel are cool and structural, precise and interesting in a way the deutzia blooms are not.

In late May or early June, a forest of mountain laurel in bloom floats on nearby Mt. Tom, turning a familiar hike into something magical. And if we're lucky here in western Massachusetts, the cool breath of a big wind will wreathe the pond water at the DAR State Park in Goshen with those same pink-and-white blossoms.

Here is how Richard Jaynes describes the inflorescence of the mountain laurel:

In some species, the flowers are solitary in the axils of the leaves, while in others they are in terminal or axillary clusters. The flowers are relatively large, varying from 0.25 to 1 in. (6 to 25 mm) in width. The calyx is five-parted and is usually persistent in fruit. The shallow, five-lobed petals are fused into a saucer-shaped corolla with a short narrow tube. Each has 10 small pouches holding the anthers. The 10 stamens have slender filaments and anthers that open by apical slits. The five-celled ovary is superior (above the calyx) . . .

Jaynes is a plant geneticist. His prose is descriptive and scientific, as befits the intent of his book.

Diane Ackerman is a poet, essayist, and naturalist. Her books of poetry and nonfiction are read around the world. Her best seller, *A Natural History of the Senses,* was made into a public television series. She holds an interdisciplinary Ph.D. from Cornell, where she has been a visiting professor.

Her work has been characterized as a marriage between art and science; it's an excellent mix for writing about plants and gardens. Here is Diane Ackerman's description of forsythia:

Spring has hit with a visual thunderclap followed by trumpet flourishes. Dazzling yellow forsythia bushes zoom all over town. Some people have planted long forsythia hedges, a clue to one's personality. First bush to bloom, forsythias gush color, their limbs flail in the wind as if on fire, and several bushes can light up a whole street. They startle in early spring by bringing clouds of gold to an overcast world . . . So forsythia really appeals to impatient, easily inflamed souls like me.

Richard Jaynes and Diane Ackerman are both garden writers. (Ackerman writes on many other subjects, as her fans know.) Worlds of difference separate the intent and purpose of Jaynes and Ackerman, yet both are garden writers of work we readers of English welcome equally.

And there are many other kinds of garden writing. Anne Raver and Ken Druse are garden writers whose articles about plants, gardens, and gardeners usually alternate on Thursdays in the *New York Times*. The feature stories they write are different in content and style from the books of either Richard Jaynes or Diane Ackerman. (Feature articles are discussed in chapter 3.) So is the work of local newspaper columnists reminding readers when it is time to plant that last crop of lettuces in August or that the autumnal deadline for the cultivation of garlic looms.

Who Is a Garden Writer?

A great canopy covers writers, professional or not, who might be considered garden writers. Even so, there are scoffers of limited understanding (and limited imagination) of the breadth and depth of what is loosely called "garden writing."

Pay no mind to those who sniff and wonder what sort of effort it takes to write about mulching tomatoes. Garden writing encompasses nonfiction writing in all of its forms. Its subjects and approaches are limitless.

Gardening, like writing, is a skill and an art practiced with infinite variety. Every gardening generation produces its crop of garden writers. Yet twenty-first-century gardeners still eagerly read the work of nineteenth-century gardeners, designers, and plant explorers. And why not? There's no expiration date on passion. Even if cultivation methods and theories of plant genetics have changed, gardeners from all times share in the same miraculous forces of nature and human desire.

Many points of view are presented by the people who write about what they've learned from plants and gardens:

- Botanists
- Horticulturists
- Plant pathologists
- Landscape designers
- Nursery owners
- Landscape maintenance people
- Master Gardeners

- Plant collectors
- Plant explorers
- Farmers
- Foresters
- Botanical garden directors and educators
- Plant- and seed-catalog writers
- Home gardeners
- Naturalists
- Anthropologists
- Archaeologists
- Ecologists
- Newspaper columnists
- Newspaper feature writers
- Newsletter writers
- Historians
- General nonfiction writers
- Fiction writers
- Travelers
- Travel writers
- Memoirists
- Artists
- Philosophers

Richard Jaynes fits into a number of the random garden-writer categories above. In *Kalmia,* he discusses, classifies, and dissects seven species and the eighty recognized cultivars. A table, for example, in the chapter titled "Micropropagation of Mountain Laurel" offers information about the amount of macro- and micronutrients that should be added to stocks of growth regulators. Botanists read and use this book; it was written by a scientist.

I am a mere home gardener and writer who will never in this lifetime propagate mountain laurel, cooking up growth compound to freeze alongside containers of homemade chicken stock.

But I love mountain laurel, and I love Richard Jaynes's book. I love looking at the pages of color photographs identifying the plant's various cultivars; I love looking up the author's description of the flowers; the drawings of their parts; and, because I have such a fine old specimen plant, pruning advice.

I love the book because it is the definitive book on mountain laurel, but most especially I love this book because someone had the training, knowledge, guts, and grand passion to follow his bliss, as it is said, for four decades. It's a fine thing to take our botany straight.

It's also a fine thing to take our botany well mixed. Diane Ackerman's book is subtitled *A Natural History of My Garden.* In its chapters, the writer romps through her garden and her life as she does through history, botany, sociology, zoology, psychology, climatology, poetry — embracing almost the whole of life and the life of our planet — with the wit and wisdom of a master storyteller. It's an irresistible read.

Most gardeners with twin passions for reading and the art and science of horticulture have books, magazines, and clippings whose writers take every possible approach to their subjects.

These written materials reflect our tastes and inclinations. I have books on cacti and succulents, on haymaking and beekeeping, on trellis making and vegetable breeding, on rock gardening and even on the gardens of Italian villas by the novelist Edith Wharton. I suspect you do too.

So what is garden writing? It is nonfiction. I think that can be agreed upon, even though there are marvelous passages by novelists (Virginia Woolf and Henry James among them) describing gardens and gardening and plants.

In most major newspapers, columns and articles about gardening appear on a certain day of the week. Some columnists focus on the "how" of gardening (damping-off, for example); others are engaged in the "why" (the motivations and passions). Henry Mitchell, who wrote for many years for the *Washington Post,* embraced both the how and the why in the books of his collected columns, as did many other writers, including Elizabeth Lawrence and Katharine White.

If you were to train yourself as a painter, you would spend time looking at paintings. As you grew in your craft, you would look at paintings to analyze color fields, the masses that make up the composition, negative space, brushstrokes, and the thickness of paint. Your discrimination would grow daily. You would choose specific artists to study.

In order to paint, you train yourself to see. In order to write, you must read with pleasure and with an ear to hearing a voice that just might resemble your own — or not. And you will begin to read as writers do, with an eye to the internal structure of a piece of writing.

Where to start? The literature of the garden is vast. You will likely start according to your need. If you have been asked to write something about your plant specialty for a weekly newspaper, you don't have time to read deeply; you have a deadline. If that's the case, see chapter 2 for models of how to write about a plant.

Otherwise, if you live in a place of seasonal gardening, winter is the time when most gardeners read about gardens. It's a way of cultivating hope, but also a way to think about what you want to plant in the next season. It can also be a time to listen to the voices of garden writers.

But whenever you find the time, read — and read deeply. You will hear the rhythm of the voices of those who feel as you do about the worlds contained within the garden. Writers are careful readers. The point is for you to see the grand arc of subjects and angles in this world of horticulture and to imagine how you might fit in.

How to Find a Subject: The Botanic Garden at Smith College

Many beginning writers find it difficult to zero in on a subject. I've often heard from students ideas ranging from the too wide ("Choosing Annuals or Perennials") to the too abstract ("Suburban Gardeners in Search of Happiness"). It's not that a skilled writer can't write about these subjects; each could be written about in a wry and humorous manner, for example. More often, however, a focused subject is best. You will more easily define, research, and write about a specific plant or a particular aspect of gardening.

If you were to visit a botanic garden such as the one at Smith College, in Northampton, Massachusetts, or Rancho Santa Ana, in Claremont, California, you might want to encourage other gardeners to do the same by writing a short piece in the newsletter of a local plant society or garden club.

In a general piece about the Botanic Garden at Smith College, for example, you would write about its location, size, and layout; the opening hours of the Lyman Conservatory; the best times of year to visit; and other information important to a casual visitor.

Include information of importance, though, to a specific audience. If you are to write for the newsletter of a dahlia society, focus on these plants and how they are displayed and used. The article should be short, readable, and to the point.

Visiting the Smith College campus will give you a range of ideas for other articles. Consider this partial list:

- Frederick Law Olmsted's 1893 master plan for the Smith campus
- History and restoration of the Lyman Conservatory
- Ecological balance of Paradise Pond and the Mill River
- Rock garden (modeled on Royal Botanical Gardens, Kew)
- Japanese garden
- Systematics garden
- Herbarium
- Perennial border next to the Lyman Conservatory
- Capen Garden, history and restoration
- Woodland Garden
- Mary Maples Dunn Garden
- President's Garden
- 150-acre arboretum
- Unusual trees (*Metasequoia glyptostroboides,* one of the largest dawn redwoods in the country, or the gorgeous Camperdown elm, *Ulmus glabra* 'Camperdownii', crowning the rock garden)
- Exhibits in the Church Exhibition Gallery, Lyman Plant House
- Fall Chrysanthemum Show
- Spring Bulb Show
- Annual lectures
- Sitting on a bench in the Palm House while snow falls
- Walking in moonlight along the river through the woodland garden

A garden writer could spend years mining the Smith campus and its rich horticultural vein. The point is that there is no end to what is contained within the idea and the reality of a botanic garden—or of any other garden. Gardens are repositories of culture, knowledge, and life.

You may be a gardener who is strictly interested in the "how" of gardening. You may want to write as technically as possible on the cultivation of old roses because it has been your passion for twenty years, but you are not trained in botany. Readers can still profit from your experience. What you owe your audience is threefold: understanding, experience, and accuracy. You must understand the audience for whom you are writing, and you must engage in direct reporting, which is the heart of journalism.

But wherever your interest in writing about plants and gardens falls within the forms of nonfiction writing, the great chorus of garden writing needs fresh voices. It's time you added yours.

CHAPTER TWO

The Straight Scoop: How to Write How-to and Service Stories

I love Wednesday. Like everyone else, I love the idea of the middle of the week, but for a reader of the *New York Times,* Wednesday means the food section. I read it religiously. I read about new restaurants, new kitchen gadgetry, food products, cookbooks, and, of course, the recipes. I read every word of the profiles of chefs from Brooklyn, Ivory Coast, Iraq, Italy, wherever. I'm on the lookout for cultural and familial influences on people committed to lives in the kitchen and to feeding others.

Most chefs grew up watching mothers, grandmothers, aunts, or fathers at the stove, stirring the stew, and there is no stew without a story—of family, of culture, of history. It's the same with gardeners.

As soon as I read the Wednesday food section in the *Times,* I tear out articles. The backbone of my small kitchen is a wide, built-in bookshelf of cookbooks, food magazines, and reference books about food and food history. I stuff these articles between books, on top of magazines, into cookbooks on similar subjects.

When I look at these stories again, a task somewhat like a treasure hunt, I'm not looking for family or culture or history. I'm hungry; I want to cook. I'm looking for recipes.

A recipe is the quintessential how-to article. It must be concise, precise, unerring: in a word, perfect. The reader of a recipe will feed the results of having read it to children, friends, spouses, partners. It's a time-sensitive responsibility. Home cooks are on a deadline called dinner hour.

A recipe writer must tell all up front: how long the recipe will take to prepare, which utensils are needed, how many people the recipe will serve. Nothing can be taken for granted.

Though I have been following recipes for thirty-five years, I still get carried away. I will fail to read a recipe all the way through and before I know it, the Mixmaster is whirring. If halfway into the recipe I read "Slice an almost stale sponge cake into three-inch pieces," I'm not going to be a happy cook.

There is a craft and a form to writing step-by-step stories, stories describing a process that the reader can follow for herself. You can learn the craft.

Why Write a How-To?

Think of the hours you have spent at dusk with a cup of tea, rapturous, looking at that new perennial bed. The silvery artemisia work perfectly. You call over your neighbor to admire your work. You are in love with the glimmering light of these plants, and your neighbor catches your enthusiasm.

That artemisia-glowing-at-dusk experience is similar to what you feel when you see an article written by your own hand about something you love. Other gardeners will see it, and some will give your passion a try. If you're writing for a newsletter or community newspaper, you'll hear about it. It's a way to make a gardening community.

The writer of a how-to article about a gardening subject is writing a recipe. The responsibility to communicate with precision and clarity is the same as that of a food-recipe writer.

Why would you, a gardener, bother to write a how-to story? Gardeners learn from other gardeners; they join groups; groups have newsletters. You may belong to the local Hemerocallis Society, the Cactus and Succulent Society, a garden club. You may be asked to write, or you may want to write, about some special knowledge you have — about desert-hardy irises or perhaps winter-hardy cacti. The hallmark of these stories is a simple, step-by-step, logical structure so that someone else can walk out into the garden and do exactly as the writer suggests.

Most how-to articles are written from the writer's own experience. But before a writer begins, he or she must understand the intended audience for the piece.

Audience and Subject

Who will be your audience? Knowing your readers is essential before you write. Articles about gardening are pitched to audiences ranging from people who are about to buy their first houseplant to those who spend their working hours in a tissue-culture lab.

"How to Buy Your First Iris Bulbs," directed toward the novice, is not the topic for the Iris Society's newsletter, but "Breeding Bearded Irises for High-Desert Blooming" would be.

If you are to write for a small publication and aren't sure of your audience, ask the editor. He or she will define the readers for you in one sentence. (For larger publications, you can find this information elsewhere, a subject discussed in chapter 8.)

If you are a member of a garden or plant-related organization and have been asked to write a how-to story for a newsletter or a bulletin, your target audience will consist of people like you. People with a strong enough interest to join the group will want to increase their knowledge. You can slant your piece to a certain level of expertise.

The Basic Elements of a How-to Article

- Title
- Headnote (introductory paragraph)
- Body (often, but not always, five or more bullet points or numbered steps of logical, sequential instructions)
- Closing paragraph

The reader should be able to follow the directions in order to achieve something close to the results you are aiming for. Here is a short how-to piece by professional gardener Eugene Lawrence, which was published in DiRT: *A Garden Journal from the Connecticut River Valley.* Eugene writes this advice to gardeners in the Northeast.

EXAMPLE

To Plant a Tree, Shrub, or Perennial

Site the plant according to sun/shade requirements. Allow ample room for at least three years' growth. Make note of the time of year, especially if you are planting in the spring and fall. How much sun will the plant receive in summer? Take the following into consideration for new plantings:

• Dig a hole the same depth as the plant container and at least twice as wide. Avoid planting it any deeper, as the plant might suffocate. Square off the hole. Edges should be perpendicular to the bottom of the hole to allow for plenty of loose soil for new roots to penetrate.

• Add any or all of the following soil amendments: compost, well-rotted cow manure, peat moss, and shredded bark mulch. They can be mixed in equal parts with the soil from the hole.

• Place the plant in the hole, checking for proper depth. Backfill the amended soil to about half full and press down the soil with your hands. Complete the backfilling and tamp down again. The soil surrounding the plant should be even with the ground.

• Create a berm around the plant at the edge of the hole to serve as a dam for water. Make sure that any leaves, in the case of a shrub or shrubby tree, that may have been buried under berm soil are freed.

• Water sufficiently to soak the soil and root-ball. Water every three or four days. Keep the plant well watered during its first year.

• Be careful: Four inches of mulch will suppress weeds, but six inches can suffocate the root system of even an established tree.

Title

Eugene's title, "To Plant a Tree, Shrub, or Perennial," is clear and concise, and leaves no doubt about the subject of his piece. Titles must always be informative.

Readers should be able to make an instant decision about whether or not to read a practical article.

Some titles may contain a bit of imaginative writing without diluting their intent. Eugene (or his editor) might have entitled his piece "Steps to Success: How to Plant a Tree, Shrub, or Perennial" or even "Recipe for Success: How to Plant . . ."

The title of this article is so clear that instead of repeating the words *tree, shrub,* and *perennial* in the body of the article, the writer refers to *plant* instead. The intent of the author, however, is not in doubt.

A writer can easily subvert the usefulness of a title. Eugene's article if entitled "Grandmother's Fail-Proof Gardening Methods" would be annoying. Readers will have to dig in to find out if the subject is of interest, or, more likely, will skip the piece altogether. (In large professional publications, the writer will not be the headline writer, by the way.)

Headnote

The headnote is a short paragraph introducing the topic. In this case, the writer begins with three quick preliminary instructions. Then he sets up the reader for what comes next: "Take the following into consideration for new plantings."

Tools or other equipment needed to complete the tasks should be mentioned in the headnote, as well as special plants or other materials. (The writer should note the plants or tools that are difficult to find and recommend where they can be purchased.) Include any caution about the process. Use short, precise sentences. Avoid abbreviations.

Body

Often, but not always, the body of a how-to piece is written using bullet or numbered points. You want the reader to bring the article out to the garden, prop it up against the fence, take spade in hand, and follow the instructions.

Parallel construction (that is, the same grammatical structure) is critical to the success of the article. The instructions in this piece begin with an action verb in the same tense: dig, add, place, create, water, and be careful.

Parallel construction of steps invites clarity and avoids confusion. If one point begins: "You should . . ." and the following step begins, "Compost and peat moss can be added," you run the risk of confusing the reader.

Instructions must be in logical order, like a recipe.

Define specialized language for the reader as you write.

Remember: no surprises! The last or next-to-last step of the process you are describing should not call for an object or anything else that hasn't been mentioned previously. No one wants to read at the end of a how-to story: "Plant bulbs in a prepared 6-foot by 6-foot bed."

Closing Paragraph

What else does your reader need to know? In Eugene's article, he explains how to water a tree during and after planting and in its first year in the ground. He also makes suggestions about successful mulching of the plant.

Format

All publications use computers. Your publisher will probably want you to submit your article "pasted" into the body of an e-mail. Ask. Don't assume anything.

What if you aren't computer literate? Then write or type your manuscript, count the words, bake some muffins, and take your article and the muffins to a computer-literate friend who will type it in for you and send it on its electronic way.

Length

Ask the editor or publisher what the exact length of your article should be. She or he will tell you in number of words. Use the word counter in your word processing software.

Narrative How-to Articles

Using bullet points in the body of the article is only one way of presenting a how-to. Another is to use a more narrative, or storytelling, approach. In this kind of article, the reader hears the "voice" of the writer and gathers an impression of the writer's personality.

The body of the story is still presented in a logical, step-by-step manner, but is organized by subheads. The process described by the writer is amplified within fully written paragraphs, and may even include brief personal and historical digressions.

The following example comes from farmer, gardener, and longtime writer Mark Adams. His weekly column, "Let's Grow," appears in a local Hudson River Valley (New York) newspaper. (In 2003, the Garden Writers Association bestowed a Garden Globe Award of Distinction on this piece.)

EXAMPLE

Reap What You Sow

Last night I baked my own bread. From wheat I grew in my own garden. The whole process from grain to bread is rife with almost biblical overtones, with mysterious and arcane references to "threshing," "flailing," and "bringing in the sheaves." And it was surprisingly easy.

Ordering the Seed

Always looking for something different to grow from seed (over the years I've tried okra, red sweet corn, parsnips, salsify, soybeans, Russian sea kale, even peanuts), I thumbed through my Johnny's Selected Seed Catalog and on a whim ordered two packets of spring wheat, the hard red variety 'Quantun', with "superior bread-baking quality." I got about 750 seeds for $3. (See johnnyseeds.com or call 800-879-2258.)

Sowing and Growing

I tilled up a 5 × 5-foot patch of garden soil, between the soybeans and cherry tomatoes, added some composted goat manure, and sowed the seed in rows 8 inches apart, probably too thickly, as I do with everything else in my tiny garden. Wheat does grow easily in Dutchess County, where thousands of acres were in production 200 years ago. (Wheat was the Hudson Valley's first major cash crop, bringing $2.75 a bushel before the Erie Canal opened in 1825.) I had my share of production headaches: a light infestation of spider mites, which must have lived on garden debris over the mild winter, then a storm that "lodged" (blew down) the stalks, and finally a tree fell on the wheat. It still grew, but it turned golden a little prematurely, in early August.

Reaping

Since the grain had lodged, I waded into my field not with scythe glinting in the sun, but carrying a pair of scissors. I cut the heads off the stalks and filled a bushel basket with them. Then came a month of "letting it dry," with Sue constantly pleading that I get the wheat off the kitchen table. "I can buy bread at Price Chopper," she kept saying.

Threshing

Now the fun began. Not having easy access to a thresher, I set about trying to shake the grain out of the seed heads. It didn't shake out, so I put the wheat in an old pillowcase and drove back and forth over it repeatedly with my car. A few kernels were dislodged, but I needed every grain of wheat possible if I was going to make a whole loaf of bread. I finally resorted to rubbing the heads vigorously between the palms of my hands for about six hours, until every last kernel was dislodged. Chaff was flying all over the house, and Sue kept saying she could buy bread at Price Chopper. I didn't believe her. I've never been to Price Chopper.

Winnowing

Another couple of weeks waiting for the wind to be just right. Now the wheat and chaff mixture filled a 10-quart pail. I put it through a sieve to get rid of some of the larger pieces of stem, and then spent a couple of more hours squeezing every last kernel out of the separated seed heads. One windy afternoon last week I went out onto the porch and started separating the wheat from the chaff by pouring it from one pail to another. By adjusting the space between the pails, I found the point at which the chaff blew away (into the pool, of course) but the heavier wheat fell into the pail below. I poured this stuff back and forth all afternoon and ended up with four cups of pure wheat (worth about three cents at current market prices).

Milling

I wanted to take my wheat down to the local mill, but that would have meant hitching up the horses, so instead I turned the Oster blender to "grind" and poured the wheat in. It ground, sort of. I poured the half-ground grain into a sifter and sifted the flour into a bowl, pouring the unground grain back into the blender. After doing this for a half hour, I ended up with four cups of rather coarse flour. It looked sort of like cornmeal, but that would have to do.

Baking the Bread

Now it was time to open my Betty Crocker Cookbook and start to rock and roll. It was 9:00 on a Thursday night, but I couldn't wait. I was pleasantly surprised that I had enough for not one but two whole loaves of bread. The baking process went smoothly, except when I had to wait for the dough to rise. (I snuck out to sing laser karaoke.) Finally, at 1:30 A.M., my golden loaves of real, homemade whole-wheat bread were ready to eat. They tasted almost as good as the bread Sue had just brought from Price Chopper.

Is "Reap" a How-to Story?

Mark Adams's piece is a step-by-step explanation of how he came to bake his own bread from wheat he grew himself. It is a how-to story. But it isn't an article that any of us could take in hand one spring day and then end up with two loaves of bread three months later. We would need more detailed instructions about growing and processing wheat.

Instead, his article is more of a narrative piece — that is, Mark employs story-telling techniques. He narrates how he came to have two "golden loaves of real, homemade whole-wheat bread" popping out of the oven at 1:30 in the morning. "Reap" is quite different in intent, structure, voice, and result from Eugene Lawrence's "To Plant" article, with its terse language and bullet points. Both kinds of how-to stories are important to the garden writer's repertoire, but each serves a different purpose.

At the heart of this storytelling is the human tale that accompanies the wheat growing and harvesting. "Reap" is a hybrid: the how-to married to a personal narrative. The story is written in the first person, the "I" of the piece. It's as if Mark Adams is driving and we are in the backseat. He's taking us on a journey.

Intent

Wheat growing and grain extraction are the boiled-down subjects of this article. The intent of the piece is something else. The subtext, or core of this story, is passion. Whether a reader will actually try to grow her own wheat and bake two loaves of bread is unknown, but I suspect that after reading this story, she will consider it. (Hmm . . . maybe a five-by-five, full-sun bed will fit over by the peonies?) The writer fell in love with what he did. The love spills out of every sentence. We can't help but feel it ourselves.

Lead Paragraph

In a narrative such as "Reap," the opening is called the lead paragraph. This is where the writer "hooks" or entices the potential reader to become an actual reader. Writing a compelling lead is an art. In a lead paragraph, the writer has no room for digression or chat or equivocation.

Mark's lead begins: "Last night I baked my own bread. From wheat I grew in my own garden." The words are direct. There is an immediate impression of almost childlike pride. The second "sentence" defies our grade-school teacher's rules of grammar, of course, but here, voice trumps all. You can "hear" the writer's voice, and the voice urges us to continue reading.

He goes on: "The whole process from grain to bread is rife with almost biblical overtones, with mysterious and arcane references to 'threshing,' 'flailing,' and 'bringing in the sheaves.' " We readers are in the hands not of a childlike enthusiast, after all, but of someone who loves language and history.

Structure

Instead of bullet points, the writer organizes his column with the use of seven very brief subheads. These are directional signs to the reader: "This paragraph is about this subject. Interested? Then read; it will take only a few seconds."

Subheads divide the article graphically as well. They are a point of entry for the reader. For some readers, subheads allow for skimming of the piece. A reader in a hurry may ask herself: What is "winnowing" anyway? She reads the "winnowing" paragraph, is intrigued, then reads the entire article.

Subheads are organized logically and chronologically. "Ordering the Seed" is the first step, "Sowing and Growing" the second, and so on to "Baking the Bread."

Over the twenty-five years that Mark has had a weekly column, he has learned that structure keeps the writer, as well as the reader, organized and focused. Some weeks, he organizes his column with subheads and narrative exposition; at other times, he is strictly a headnote–bullet point–endnote man.

Voice and Tone

Voice is how the writer speaks on the page and the impression of the writer that is made in the reader's mind. Voice has to do with vocabulary and rhythm and structure — and above all, tone, which may range from humor to hyperbole to solemnity.

Listen to this sentence: "Last night I baked my own bread from wheat I grew in my own garden." The sentence is grammatically correct. It's fine. The sentence is in a lead paragraph, however, and the reader doesn't hear anything special in these acts of baking and growing. We don't hear much of the unique voice of the writer.

But crack a grammar rule and suddenly we readers of "Reap" can "hear" something of what will follow in the story: "Last night I baked my own bread." That emphatic full stop. "From wheat I grew in my own garden." That's pride we hear in the growing of the wheat. Understated pride and humor will take us through this piece from the buying of seed to the baking of bread.

"And it was surprisingly easy," he writes. It was no such thing, and he quickly proves it. But the writer's enthusiasm, coupled with his signature understatement, makes it seem as if it was. Delicious hyperbole (exaggeration pushed to make a point) peeks around almost every corner of this piece.

Mark's sly, wry humor is evident in the article, and is a hallmark of his voice. In his columns, he often sets up "Sue" (his wife; he doesn't tell us who she is, but we can guess) as a foil for his humor. Here, Sue's skepticism, common sense, and devotion to Price Chopper bread are in delightful contrast to Mark's naughty-boy persona: He hogs the kitchen table; causes chaff to fly all over the house; runs over the wheat with his car; on the perfect windy day, he winnows the wheat, sending the chaff into the pool. In between, Mark manages to give us a brief history of wheat growing in the Hudson River Valley and the market price for the four cups of wheat he eventually produces in a summer of hard work.

The tone of a writer's voice can be formal or informal, scholarly or chatty, serious or humorous. Mark's tone is: Let me tell it to you straight. Of course he doesn't tell it straight (did he really run over a pillowcase stuffed with wheat in his car?). Hyperbole makes him fun to read. In the end, he punctures what he has inflated — his pride in growing and reaping and threshing and engaging in all those great biblical verbs.

His voice is authentic, lively, and humorous. His credentials as a professional gardener and grower are unassailable, yet he convinces the rest of us that we, too, can grow wheat and bake our own bread — in the middle of the night, if we can tear ourselves away from laser karaoke.

Service Story

Let's suppose you have two or three clear, concise, and successful how-to stories under your writing belt. How-to stories typically describe steps in a process. A "service" article is another type of article that will be of help to the reader. Think of it as a "ready-to-use" article. Information is conveyed simply and quickly to the reader, but the information is different from that of a simple how-to story.

What will you do? How will you start? Writers obtain accurate information in a number of ways. The following may seem obvious, but if you're in a hurry, a checklist is helpful.

Information Sources for Garden Writers

- Books
- Magazines and newsletters
- Newspapers
- Internet
- Interviews with experts
- Interviews with amateurs

Rules for Using Printed Sources

1. Take accurate notes about all publications you consult: name of author(s); title; page number(s); date and place of publication.
2. Copy the information verbatim; use quotation marks in your notes; photocopying may be more efficient.
3. Consult professional publications. Newsletters from plant societies and botanical gardens are good sources of material. A neighborhood newsletter may have a charming article about blue poppies, but you can't count on accuracy.
4. If you quote a printed source, you must use quotation marks and cite the source of the material.
5. If you are paraphrasing material, you must still acknowledge the source.

Rules for Using Internet Sources

Many of the same rules for using printed sources apply. In addition:

- Make a note of the address of the Web site you are consulting.
- Look at the source of the Web site. Inaccurate information abounds on the Web. A chat-room posting about a plant is not a source of accurate information. Instead, look for sites hosted by botanical gardens and plant societies. A general site, such as www.gardenweb.com, can direct you to a professional site. Purveyors of plants and seeds on the Web are often, but not always, a source of accurate information.
- If you are using the words of a site verbatim, use quotation marks around the information and cite the Web site's address.
- If you are paraphrasing the information, you still must acknowledge the source.

EXAMPLE

In this example of a service story, Erica Browne Grivas, a former writer for the New York Botanical Garden, presents lively and interesting information about new, cold-hardy plants that many cold-climate gardeners may not know are available in their USDA Zones. Erica wrote this for the online DiRT: *A Garden Journal from the Connecticut River Valley.*

Out of the West Come More Reliable, Cold-Hardy Hyssops

People are blazing a trail west to find the newest hyssops, and it's easy to see why. These southwestern natives boast sun-kissed colors, easygoing natures, delightfully fragrant leaves and flowers, and a substantial bloom time to boot.

Mint Family
Commonly known as "hyssops" or "giant hyssops," these plants are distinct from the true hyssop, *Hyssopus officinalis.* They are the agastaches, a broad genus of about 30 species in the mint family,

native mainly to North America and Mexico.

An Internet search reveals the versatility of the agastaches: They are used in herbal teas, butterfly gardens, and xeriscapes. Their unwieldy name (a-gah-STAH-kee) comes from the Greek *aga,* meaning "very much," and *stachys,* meaning "ears of wheat."

Gardeners have known since the 1800s about *Agastache foeniculum,* the anise or giant blue hyssop, a half-hardy perennial herb with licorice-scented leaves. But this mint family group also includes lesser-known agastaches that are making breeders and gardeners take notice. These, according to one hybridizer, boast greater hardiness than anise hyssop, as well as diversity of color and fragrance.

While anise hyssop sports blue flowers, these agastaches speak in bolder tones — raspberry pink, apricot, cerise, and burnt orange. They exude fragrances that mimic not only mint, but also root beer, licorice, bubble gum, and combinations thereof.

Noninvasive

Agastaches are clump-forming rather than stoloniferous, and will not romp through the garden like certain of their rowdier mint cousins. Blooming in mid- to late summer, they range in height from about 18 inches *(A. 'Firebird')* to 5 feet *(A. barberi).* The common name of the latter, giant hummingbird mint, speaks to another attribute — they are irresistible to hummingbirds.

"[Anise hyssop] is the least interesting and the most commonly available," says David Salman, president and chief horticulturist of Santa Fe Greenhouses Inc., in New Mexico. Thanks to Salman and other agastache fans, that may be changing. He now sells eight named agastache cultivars through High Country Gardens, the company's catalog division, and is busily hybridizing them.

Undemanding and Resilient

In culture, these plants are undemanding and resilient, preferring conditions similar to those of lavenders: full sun, well-drained soil, perhaps topped by gravel mulch. Like lavenders, their weakness is the double whammy of heat and humidity found in the Southeast, but they do well in most other regions, including the Northeast, especially with good drainage and sun. Salman's New York and Pennsylvania customers have reported success growing them near a sunny wall. Some varieties that he has found adaptable to moister garden soil are *A. cana* and *A.* 'Firebird'. In Zone 4, agastaches are fine annuals. Propagate agastaches either from stem cuttings or by seed.

Hardy and Interesting Cultivars

1. *Agastache* × 'Blue Fortune' grows 2–3 feet, with powder blue flower spikes. Excellent butterfly and bee plant, long blooming, widely adaptable. Recommended for eastern gardens. Zones 6 through 9.
2. *A. rupestris* (sunset hyssop) smells like a combination of root beer and licorice. Deep orange flower, to 2 feet. Blooms for up to 10 weeks. Zones 5 through 9.
3. *A. cana;* sweet fragrance, like bubble gum. Two to 3 feet, rose-purple flowers for about 6 weeks. Zones 5 through 9.
4. *A. aurantiaca* (Jewel of the Sierra Madres) has soft orange flowers, minty foliage; approximately 2 feet. Zones 6 through 9.
5. *A. barberi* (giant hummingbird mint) sports bright pink flowers, up to 5 feet in height. Zones 5 through 9.
6. *A.* 'Firebird' grows to 18 inches. Long blooming, with orange-scarlet flowers; adaptable to heavier garden soils. Zones 8 and 9.

Where to Buy Plants

High Country Gardens
2902 Ruffina Street
Santa Fe, NM 87505
800-925-9387; www.highcountrygardens.com

Heronswood Nursery
7530 NE 288th Street
Kingston, WA 98346
360-297-4172; www.heronswood.com

Plant Delights Nursery, Inc.
919-772-4794; www.plantdelights.com

Where to Buy Seeds

Rocky Mountain Rare Plants
1706 Deerpath Road
Franktown, CO 80116
www.rmrp.com

Intent and Tone of "Out of the West"

Erica's intent in writing this story is one common to writer-gardeners: She wants to cultivate delight in her readers. She has fallen in love with a plant. She wants to share that joy with other gardeners. The cheerful tone of the piece communicates the writer's enthusiasm.

Sometimes the falling in love is reversed. You could be asked to write something for your organization's newsletter about a plant you barely know and have never grown yourself. You begin to research the plant, you take a good look at it, love blossoms. Then a hopeful flatful is teetering on the backseat of your Subaru. (It's a happy occupational hazard, but don't ask me about my three dozen *Festuca glauca*.)

Title

Erica's title, "Out of the West Come More Reliable, Cold-Hardy Hyssops," is descriptive, newsworthy, and sly. The article is about hyssops; it is newsworthy in that the writer is reporting on new hybrids that will be more reliable in colder climates than previously available cultivars of the plants. But sly? Yes. Many gardeners, at some point in their gardening history, flirt with zone denial. That is, we want to grow what allegedly can't be grown where we live, whether USDA Zone 5 or Zone 9. More reliable cold-hardy hyssops? Hmm . . .

Lead

The lead of Erica's article is designed to "hook," or draw in, her reader. Erica has written thirty-seven words in two sentences, which make up a short paragraph.

You should write and rewrite and think about your lead as if each word were worth, say, a thousand dollars. It is your one chance to say to the reader: *I'm going to take you on an adventure. Come along!*

Let's look at Erica's lead: "People are blazing a trail west to find the newest hyssops, and it's easy to see why." The voice is upbeat, sweeping the reader into the world of these plants. Then the writer comes in for the capture, using descriptive language that few gardeners can resist: "sun-kissed colors"; "easygoing natures"; "delightfully fragrant"; "substantial bloom time."

Structure

The best service stories are simple, quick to read, and visually interesting. "Out of the West" is structured to give detailed but succinct information about agastaches. The writer is simplifying the information to serve the busy reader. This is the structure of this piece: eight paragraphs, a six-point list, four subheads, and a sidebar.

Here are the ten elements that make up this story:
- Lead
- Plant identification
- Uses of the plant
- History
- Color/attractiveness to insects
- Invasiveness
- Quotation from expert

- Cultivation information
- List of recommended hybrids
- Sidebar: Where to buy plants and seeds

Each paragraph is no more than four sentences. Why is this? In a service article, the reader wants concise information. The writer is mindful of the reader's time. The service article is not the place to write long paragraphs about childhood memories of agastaches, although a single sentence on the subject might be fine.

You can use the list above as a template for an article of your own. This is not cheating or plagiarism. It is important for you to learn to crack the code of an article — that is, to read for structure. This will help you to write clearly and concisely. Copy this page and tape it up near your desk. Practice. Service articles aren't novels or works of contemplation. Learn the structure.

Write as if you were speaking directly to a reader, and, as in any nonfiction article, define your audience before you begin. "Out of the West" is for home gardeners. If it was written for a retailer or nursery grower, the piece would be far more technical. A grower needs precise information on greenhouse cultivation: growing medium, temperature, and seed germination and other propagation methods, such as tissue culture.

Sources of Botanical Information for Plant Identification

Finding a good source of accurate botanical information about a plant can be tricky. Use Internet sources with caution; misinformation abounds.

A garden writer does not want to make an error in plant identification. On the other hand, the classification of a plant sometimes changes, and new hybrids are named daily. So what's a writer to do? Break down family, genus, species, cultivars, and named varieties. Most important are genus (plural: genera) and species.

One reliable source for plant identification is the International Plant Names Index. See the resources section at the back of this book for others.

Information: Quoted, Summarized, or Paraphrased?

Erica has identified three sources of information for this article. She cites "Internet research" when she mentions the versatility of agastaches; she summarizes what she has read about the hardiness of the new hybrids, citing "one hybridizer"; she also quotes David Salman, of Santa Fe Greenhouses.

For a beginning writer of articles, the question of when to quote directly, when to summarize, and when to paraphrase (that is, citing the source but rewording what he or she said) can be a matter of some confusion.

When an interviewed source is giving you information that is a matter of common knowledge, it's best to summarize. The same advice applies to written and online sources.

For example, Erica writes: " 'hyssops' or 'giant' hyssops . . . are distinct from the true hyssop, *Hyssopus officinalis.* They are agastaches, a broad genus of about 30 plant species in the mint family." This is basic information about the plant that can be found almost anywhere. The reader doesn't need to know the source of this common knowledge; he or she wants to move through this information quickly. Erica has summarized what she has learned.

The information about the hardiness of some new hybrids, however, is a different matter. Erica cites the source of this information in a general way: "according to one hybridizer."

But Erica's article would be weak without directly quoting an expert. We readers want to know what a professional has to say. That's where David Salman comes in. He is the "creator" of some of these plants. He knows what he's talking about. The fact that he is actually a horticulturist and not just a businessman makes a difference. (Often, service articles have at least two "experts" weighing in on the subject.)

It's not the writer's job to rewrite quotations, but it is the writer's job to choose the liveliest and most useful ones.

When you read an article you admire, make note of the quotations. Most likely the quotations were chosen to reveal a special expertise or, in the case of a feature article, to reveal the voice and character of the interviewee.

Serving the Reader: List and Sidebar

"Out of the West" serves the reader in every paragraph and section. Look again at the list of the elements that make up the article. Erica has given us succinct information about agastaches, from history to cultivation. But what if a reader has taken in the lead paragraph (those sun-kissed colors!), has already fallen in love with the plants, and wants to order them right away?

The service story serves the reader-in-a-hurry by its very structure. A gardener can move through the piece quickly, taking in the menu of plant choices to find what will work in her garden. Then she can scan the sidebar, pick up the phone or turn on the computer, and the plants will be hers.

CHAPTER THREE

Coaxing Subjects and Characters to Life: Feature Stories

A feature story appearing in the "hard-news" section of a newspaper is often an amplification of another story. When a reporter, as opposed to a feature writer, covers breaking news — a hurricane in Florida, for example — she reports on the who, what, where, when, and how of the storm. The report may include statistics quantifying the damage caused by the storm; it will not include what the storm means on a personal level to individual victims except in a cursory way, nor will the reporter venture her own interpretation or opinion. That would be the job of a feature story writer.

A feature writer would seek out a specific, personal story to illuminate the effects of the hurricane. The piece might be layered with the human costs of the storm. The writer's opinion, although not stated as such, may be inferred.

A feature article about a garden or a gardener is not usually tied to breaking news, but it is possible. A hurricane might destroy a botanical garden, for example, or a famously beautiful park.

In early September 2004, Hurricane Frances wreaked havoc on an exclusive horticultural and residential paradise of the super-rich, Jupiter Island, Florida. A *New York Times* writer, Felicity Barringer, wrote a feature article headlined "On Jupiter Island, Storm Took Heavy Toll on Residents' Seclusion." The article appeared on September 9.

The title suggests a horticultural or other threatening problem, but not one of homelessness or loss of life. The reporter mentions in the second paragraph that the Jupiter Island ZIP code is the wealthiest neighborhood in the nation. The average price of a home on Jupiter Island is $5.6 million. Barringer writes:

> Roses were blown from their beds. Coconut palms scattered fronds, coconuts and serrated trunks everywhere. Felled banyan and seagrape, not to mention oak and pine trees, littered driveways. Cocoplum hedges were shredded.

After the following delicious quote from a landscaper, the story is off:

> "The walls are down at Jupiter Island," said Ghada Dergham, the proprietor at Jupiter Island Landscape, who planted or hung many of the orchids and ficus that are now gone. "They can see each other. That will drive them crazy."

(You can read the article, for a small fee, on www.nyt.com.)

A straight news story would give the facts — 60 percent of the shrubbery was blown away by the hurricane, for example. This is a somewhat tongue-in-cheek story that appeared in the front section of the newspaper because it was tied to breaking news. But feature articles about gardens, food, and travel usually appear in their own sections in newspapers and general-interest magazines. In some quarters, they are called human interest or enterprise stories.

A profile is a special form of the feature story. A feature may be about a subject — biodynamic gardening, perhaps — and may include interviews with at least two gardeners who use this method. A profile, however, is one person's story, or the story of a single place or entity. In a profile of a person, the writer attempts to pierce the persona of the subject to get to the motivation behind his or her actions and interests.

Profiles and other feature articles can be layered and complex pieces of reporting and writing. What they all share is that a subject is "featured"—that is, a subject is more fully explicated through an exploration of its background, meaning, complications, roots, and what may happen in the future. As in any other craft or art, feature articles are written by writers with varying levels of skill and experience. Features can be competent (or not) or they can be works of art.

How a Feature Article Is Constructed

A feature article is an engineered piece of writing. Once you get the hang of analyzing the elements of an article, you can read a feature and "see" how it is made.

Careful reading of features will be invaluable to you. You will be looking at how the writer uses the tools of the craft. Borrowing these tools for your own article isn't cheating. All writers and artists use models. If you borrow a model, you aren't borrowing words or ideas. You are modeling a framework.

A writer of features finds interesting subjects, observes, listens, asks questions, researches, and writes. Seems simple enough. Put your hands on the keyboard and out comes an article.

But here's the tricky part. You know that when you put your hands on a piece of wood and a chisel, you are unlikely to come up with an elegant and fluid sculpture unless you have apprenticed yourself to the craft and art of woodworking. You have to study and practice for years. It's the same with writing. As Ray Bradbury has written, "The artist must work so hard, so long, that a brain develops and lives, all of itself, in his fingers."

Even though you may have written a master's thesis or a technical book and have read hundreds of articles, the writing of a feature story is another matter. You can learn to do it, but you first must be able to recognize the form. Learn to read as a writer does. Learn to use a wrench to loosen the bolts of a story, to see how it is made.

Basic Elements of the Feature Story

Here are some of the elements that make up a feature story. How they are manifested within an article can be as varied as writers themselves.

- Theme
- Frame (how the story is told)
- Lead paragraph
- Nut graf

- Linked material
- Transitions (segues between sentences, paragraphs, and topics)

Theme

Every article has a theme. It is what the story is really about. Often writers don't know exactly what their theme is until they have written a first draft. When the theme emerges, the writer can rework the piece with renewed vigor as she shapes the information in the story to emphasize and reinforce the theme.

In an article about a dedicated *Meconopsis* gardener, for example, the writer may discover a gardener with deep personal losses. The resulting character-driven piece wouldn't shrink from the crucial details of growing blue poppies, but the theme of the story may be emotional survival.

Frame

In a good feature story, the writer is engaged on a voyage of discovery about the subject. She brings the adventure to life and shares it with the reader.

A feature by Anne Raver, entitled "In the Desert, Finding Blooms That Heal," appeared in the *New York Times* on March 30, 2000. On one level, it's about the native plants traditionally eaten by the O'odham people of southern Arizona. But it's also about the scourges of diabetes and alcoholism among the O'odham and their relationship with another group of Native Americans, the Seri.

The frame — that is, the organizing principle from which the writer tells the story — is a literal journey Anne Raver took with a group of O'odham and others. She accompanied (at least for a while) forty people — "desert pilgrims" — who walked 240 miles across the desert to follow the path of their ancestors. The group camped along the way and ate only desert plants in an effort to bring attention to the epidemic of diabetes affecting the tribe.

The article is about plants, ethnology, travel, ethnobiology, food, disease, history. Is it a piece of garden writing? Of course. Its subject is, in part, about the healing plants of the desert. Yet Raver's article is unforgettable first because of its frame, the actual journey in the desert, and second for the compassion and respect she has for her subjects. Anne Raver's feelings are delivered with subtlety, a hallmark of this talented writer. (You can read this article, too, for a small fee: www.nyt.com.)

Lead Paragraph

As in any nonfiction article, every word of a lead paragraph must meet the gold standard. After a few sentences, the reader should be intrigued enough to stop what he or she is doing to read on. As with the leads of how-to and any other article, this paragraph is no place for digression, chat, equivocation, or bits of self-indulgence or self-regard.

The lead paragraph of a feature is often a small work of art, but one as shrewdly as it is artistically crafted. The lead can be a stunning writerly perform-ance with a payoff in the story, at the end or elsewhere.

Nut Graf

The nut graf is usually the second paragraph of an article. It gives the grounding details of what the article will be about. This is the meaning of the term: *Nut* is the kernel, or the essence, of the article; *graf* is journalese for paragraph.

The nut graf often delivers the theme or focus of an article. Then it is the writer's responsibility to develop the theme in the paragraphs that follow.

Linked Material

Good organization is critical to a feature story. I wrote a story about *Festuca glauca* (blue fescue, an ornamental grass) for which I interviewed the renowned plantsman Kurt Bluemel. He told me that his fifty-year love affair with orna-mental grasses began when he was a young apprentice in a nursery outside Zurich. A piece of *Festuca glauca* fell off a specimen. He picked it up, planted it, and found his life's work.

In the article, this information appears together. The material is linked by theme (life's work), time (fifty years ago), and place (Zurich). If I had left out the fact that Bluemel had been a young nursery apprentice and then mentioned it elsewhere in the story, it would throw the reader off track.

When you have written a draft of a story, the search for like material is a good way to begin to organize and edit. (To find this article, visit www.dirtagarden-journal.com.)

Transitions

Often, gardeners (and others) new to writing haven't mastered the art of the transitional sentence or the transitional paragraph. Our goal is to lead readers from one paragraph to another, especially when the subject is changing, with a gentle hint of what is to come. Otherwise, the reader is stopped short.

In "Festucas," the fourth paragraph ends this way:

> When Kurt Bluemel came to the United States to work at Bluemont Nursery in 1960, he and Richard Simon began to import 30 varieties of ornamental grasses from Switzerland.

The fifth paragraph beings with this quote:

> "Coming to the United States was a cultural and horticultural shock," says Bluemel.

The information preceding the direct quote is a transition to it. Readers have been tipped off as to what Bluemel is speaking about.

Devices Borrowed from Fiction

When the novel was born, centuries ago, writers of the new genre borrowed structure and techniques from the ancient art of the theater.

Nonfiction writers in this country began borrowing writing techniques from novelists about fifty years ago. Writing teachers of all genres admonish students: Show, don't tell. What they mean is to bring characters and action to the eyes and minds of readers, something that summarizing can't do. Writing can burst into life on the page when readers see characters in action, when they can hear characters speak, when they can see them interact with their environment.

The following are usually considered narrative, or storytelling, devices that have been borrowed from fiction.

- Characterization
- Dialogue
- Setting
- Scenes
- Point of view
- Description and detail

Characterization in nonfiction is related to that in fiction — a writer is bringing a person to life on the page in all her dimensions, or at least in the dimensions that have been revealed to the writer. Characterization is essential to a lively and interesting article. People like to read about other people. Readers want to understand the subjects of articles and to speculate how they are like or unlike them. Character-driven articles can still deliver all the information necessary about cultivating delphiniums, for example, but when readers relate to the delphinium cultivator, the writer enlarges the reading experience.

Dialogue is when we hear subjects speak in their own voices and interact with one another. Dialogue is written in its own form, and is enclosed by quotation marks:

"Do you think we might tear down this wall?" Ms. Trug asked her husband.

"My grandfather built that wall," he said.

A vivid writer conveys the setting of a story in a way that the reader can see, smell, hear, and feel a place or landscape — and imagine it as if she is present in it herself. Writers often pay such sharp attention to place that it becomes as important as a main character. Think of Miss Havisham's house in *Great Expectations*. Or the lake in Marilynne Robinson's novel *Housekeeping*. (For a further discussion about writing about place, see chapter 5.)

Playwrights and screenwriters write in scenes. Theatergoers see plays one scene at a time. In a scene the actors are on stage and the stage is set with meaningful décor and objects. The actors speak to each other in dialogue. The actors move their bodies. The scene has a purpose in the play — that is, to move the action forward and to reinforce the theme of the play, the work's central idea. The opposite of a scene is the summary. This is telling, not showing. But are summaries important? Absolutely. The nonfiction writer uses a balance of scenes and summaries.

Most often a short feature article will have space for only one scene, and most other information is conveyed in summary. This scene must be carefully chosen and instructive. In longer features, such as the profiles in the *New Yorker,* the writer will show the subject in action in several scenes.

Point of view refers to the choice the writer has made to tell the story in the first (I), second (you), or third (neutral) point of view. Overuse of the first person is annoying to readers when the subject of an article is someone or something other than the writer, which it almost always is. Use the first person sparingly. (Yet some situations require the first-person pronoun — columnists always use it, and some publications require it.)

The use of the second person is difficult to pull off in an article of any sort — feature or how-to. The use of *you* to address the reader directly can sound precious, cloying, too folksy, or didactic. (Some writers, though, can pull it off beautifully.) The use of the second person in this book was a difficult decision, but as you can see, second person is in play.

In feature stories about gardens and plants, writers may use a judicious mix of first- and third-person points of view. (Anne Raver often uses just a single first-person pronoun.) Third person is what reporting is about. It is the point of view from which most news articles and feature stories are written, simply describing what "it," "she," "he," or "they" did. Readers want to think that the reporter is as unbiased as possible. (A variation employs *one* as in "one knows the consequences of planting too early in the season," but this suggests a tone and attitude one can do without.)

But here is where the writer of articles about plants and gardens can have fun. Writers can, and do, compose witty and opinionated articles without the appearance of the dreaded first-person pronoun. You can hear the voice of a writer in third person. It's called the implied first-person point of view. Felicity Barringer's piece on Jupiter Island is an example. It's a wry piece on hurricane damage, a rarity, and enjoyable because of the writer's voice, delivered through the implied first-person point of view.

In every piece of journalism, a writer has made a decision about point of view. You can master the skill of recognizing these choices. Notice the point of view of everything you read. It will help you make your own decisions about writing.

Rich description brings life to a story, as can the smallest detail. Experienced writers can often bring a person and situation to life with a single descriptive note. It's easy to overlook this skill when reading the work of others because the detail may seem obvious. A writer doesn't choose these elements at random. A single observation can summarize a character. Think of Miss Havisham's wedding dress.

Narrative or "Dam-Building" Techniques

How information in an article is delivered on the page to the reader is critical.

I once read that a feature article might be imagined as a river dammed at certain points along its way to the sea. The placement of the dams tells the reader what the writer considers important in the story — the writer is asking the reader to stop and ponder the pooling water. If the writer didn't offer these resting spots, the reader wouldn't know what is most significant about the story or what to make of the information given.

The way a writer presents information determines how the piece is read. The writer highlights what is important and interesting to underscore her theme. The writer does this, in part, by the amount of information given on a certain aspect of the story.

Writers have a number of other techniques up their sleeves intended to keep their readers awake. Writers mix the ways information is delivered. You can observe the mix in the piece as a whole and within paragraphs.

Here's a reminder of how a writer can vary the way she conveys information to emphasize what is important to the theme of the story.

- manipulation of time
- variation of sentence structure
- direct observation
- quotations from interviewees
- quotations from printed sources
- summarized material from interviewees and printed (or other) sources

- quoted or summarized observations of others
- commentary and analysis
- speculation on the future

Feature writers often don't have the space to tell a linear story. Thank goodness. The play of *time* in an article is a critical tool in the writer's repertoire of skills. An article may begin in the present or the deep past or the recent past. Writers can zip around in time to build stories, as long as there is a purpose in so doing and the reader doesn't become confused.

In the article about Jupiter Island and Hurricane Frances, the period of time the article covers is specific and limited. The writer is reporting on what happened to the landscaped areas around the houses due to the storm.

If the article was about the history of the island and how the wealthy happened to build houses there, the story would likely zoom around in time.

Short *sentences* grab a reader's attention. Longer sentences can be used to good effect, especially when followed by short ones. Varying the length of sentences is one way to speed up or slow down the flow of the narrative. Variety in length and structure is the key. Do most of your sentences begin with article adjectives (*a, an,* or *the*)? Recast them.

Direct observation is the heart of journalism. If you write an article solely from telephone interviews, you can't deliver the immediacy of direct reporting. The reader is counting on you to report and interpret what you have seen and heard.

Quotations from the people you have interviewed serve several purposes. They convey information. Carefully chosen quotations add texture and interest. They help develop characterization. (If you use quotations from printed material about your subject, you must note the source.) Most important, direct quotations allow people to speak in their own voices.

Summarized material is used to vary the way information is conveyed. Not everything your interviewee says is interesting, although the material may be crucial to the understanding of the topic of the article. The writer summarizes the material. Likewise, if the writer has researched facts about delphiniums, this information is given to the reader in summary.

Feature stories need outside corroboration. If you are writing an article for a major newspaper on a master rosarian, for example, you need to include other opinions about your subject. Two other people—another rosarian and, if appropriate, a customer of your subject—should be interviewed. You will then make the decision when to *quote* or *summarize* the information you have. You will make the same decisions regarding material from a printed or electronic source.

Commentary and *analysis* by the writer is another way to deliver information to the reader. The writer comments on information, often synthesizing it for the reader. The writer analyzes a situation, offering possible interpretations. She expresses her opinions in subtle ways. This is one of the great pleasures of writing nonfiction narratives. The writer is the decision maker behind the photographic lens. She decides what to frame, what to include and exclude, the depth of the shading in the left corner. In the end, we are seeing what she wants us to see.

Many feature stories include a brief look into the plans of the person or entity that is the subject of the story. Readers want to know what the *future* might hold. It must be part of what makes us human — wanting to speculate on what we really cannot know.

EXAMPLE

The following is an example of a feature story I wrote for the *New York Times,* which appeared August 29, 2002. (The use of the word *cactuses* was an editorial decision by the *Times. Cacti* is the usual form. Please note also that the *New York Times* and most other newspapers do not use italics for botanical names.)

Turning Cactuses into Connecticut Yankees

MIDDLEBURY, Conn. — "After all these years," John Spain said, "people still ask me if I dig up the cactus and bring them in for the winter." Mr. Spain, 81, is the Luther Burbank of winter-hardy cactuses in the Northeast. A self-taught expert who has nearly 30 varieties in his garden, he has become a quiet proselytizer for the joys of growing cactuses where Gila monsters fear to tread.

Mr. Spain's cactus-growing in Michigan and here in an

800-square-foot bed in central Connecticut led to his "Growing Winter Hardy Cacti in Cold/Wet Climate Conditions" (Elizabeth Harmon, 1997), a concise guide. "I didn't dare write it until I had at least 30 years growing experience," he said.

Most winter-hardy cactuses thrive in the dry, high, windy Rocky Mountains, where the altitude ranges from about 7,000 to 10,000 feet. "The conditions in Colorado are different, of course, but they are just similar enough so that almost every species I've found there will grow here in the Northeast," he said.

On his just-under-an-acre suburban lot, Mr. Spain has built a 110-foot south-facing rock garden, which is about 15 percent hardy cactuses and winter-tolerant succulents like yucca and agaves. (Technically, a cactus is a succulent, but not all succulents are cactuses.) He also has an apple orchard, a woodland garden, and, in a 32-foot-long greenhouse, an enormous collection of nonhardy cactuses and succulents.

Winter-hardy cactuses seem especially attractive at a time when drought plagues the Northeast. The padded and low-growing Opuntia, commonly called prickly pear, is the best known of this tolerant bunch. Cylindropuntia, or cholla, is bushier, taller and more vertical. Coryphantha are what most people call ball or barrel cactuses. Echinocereus have short and heavy starburst spines. Pediocactus, a true round shape, is the first to bloom in spring. The cactuses bloom, a few at a time, from around the first of June to mid-August. Most of the 25 species Mr. Spain recommends in his book are hardy to Zone 5, some to Zone 4.

Mr. Spain recommends that beginners grow hardy cactuses in containers, because they grow faster when corralled. He prefers containers made of hypertufa, a concrete mixture, or ordinary concrete, because conventional terra cotta pots have a tendency to crack in cold weather. When asked how many times one should water a cactus newly planted in a container, he replied, "Oh, maybe once."

Of the five requirements for successful cactus growing in wet and cold climates, the first three, he is fond of saying, are "drainage, drainage, drainage." The others are location, planting medium (sandy), top dressing (tiny pebbles) and fertilization (minimal). Location means a place receiving at least five hours of sun a day. Don't have a sunny enough spot? Plant next to rocks or boulders that reflect light. No walls, steep banks or rock out-croppings? Have a truckload of sand dumped in the backyard and mounded up three or four feet high. Hardy cactuses can be safely planted in the Northeast until Sept. 15.

Mr. Spain's love of plants dates back to childhood. His father was a dedicated camellia grower in Memphis. He had planned to become a landscape architect but instead served as a pilot with the Flying Tigers in World War II. He married, fathered three boys and worked for 40 years as an executive at Uniroyal, much of that time in Detroit. He began collecting cactuses around 1962 when he picked up a box of them at the Denver airport.

"They turned out to fascinate me," he said. Cactuses also suited his harried life. He traveled constantly, and his wife wasn't interested in gardening — or watering. He joined a cactus and succulent society, and discovered hardy cactuses through Claude A. Barr, a self-trained botanist and commercial grower in Smithwick, S.D. Mr. Spain still has cactuses descended from Mr. Barr's plants.

Jeff Rankin, a gardener at the Botanic Garden at Smith College in Northampton, Mass., considers Mr. Spain a hero. "He is truly the expert on these plants," Mr. Rankin says. Mr. Spain donated a number of hardy cactuses to Smith in the early 1990s and they now reside in a thriving cactus bed.

Joseph Gruszczak, an architectural designer who gardens on his 42-acre Connecticut estate, is another convert to cactuses. "I got stuck by the prickly pear," Mr. Gruszczak said. "I was taken to see John's garden, and the love affair began." About five years ago,

Mr. Grusczak and his partner, Bill DeGraff, landscaped a blue-stone terrace with two long meandering and intertwining beds of hardy cactuses and succulents.

These days, Mr. Spain speaks at rock garden and cactus and succulent societies and is experimenting in his greenhouse with a hardy succulent, a form of ice plant he is growing from seed collected in the mountains of South Africa. Next spring he will set out his flats of tiny new cactuses and succulents and begin to harden them off, readying them for their permanent home in his year-round beds. "I guess I'm a just a farmer at heart," he said. "I just like to grow stuff."

Let's look at the six main elements of a feature story as illustrated by this article:

Theme

I recall the tension I felt when writing this twelve-hundred-word article (edited down to just under a thousand by the *Times*). I wanted to portray the personality of the interesting Mr. Spain, but at the same time to explain the nature of winter-hardy cacti, plants most readers of the *Times* would find unfamiliar. The revelation that gardeners in the Northeast can grow these unusual and unexpectedly compliant plants was the point of the story.

Frame

A physical journey by the writer to a garden is an important and often used frame of a story about gardens and plants. Showing a character in action implies the presence of the writer. The article begins with Mr. Spain on stage.

Lead

In "Cactuses," I chose to lead into the story with a quotation from the subject. Mr. Spain's quote encapsulates the puzzlement of most northeastern gardeners when they encounter cacti in the ground.

The direct quotation also implies that the writer was there in the garden with the subject, looking at the plants with him.

> "After all these years," John Spain said, "people still ask me if I dig up the cactus and bring them in for the winter." Mr. Spain, 81, is the Luther Burbank of winter-hardy cactuses in the Northeast. A self-taught expert who has nearly 30 varieties in his garden, he has become a quiet proselytizer for the joys of growing cactuses where Gila monsters fear to tread.

After the quotation, the lens, so to speak, pulls back to put Mr. Spain in context. He is eighty-one years old, the "Luther Burbank" of winter-hardy cacti, a "self-taught expert," a "quiet proselytizer," and someone who grows thirty varieties. It's a lot of information packed into a paragraph. Not a word to spare (thanks to the shrewd editors of the *Times*).

Nut Graf

A nut graf, as mentioned earlier, grounds the reader into the essential information of the story and contains the main theme of the article. In "Cactuses," there are two nut grafs. One establishes Mr. Spain as the expert on winter-hardy cacti (important, because he is, technically speaking, in our over-credentialed world, an amateur); the other establishes the nature of these plants, something most readers would not know.

> Mr. Spain's cactus-growing in Michigan and here in an 800-square-foot bed in central Connecticut led to his "'Growing Winter Hardy Cacti in Cold/Wet Climate Conditions'" (Elizabeth Harmon, 1997), a concise guide. "I didn't dare write it until I had at least 30 years growing experience," he said.
>
> Most winter-hardy cactuses thrive in the dry, high, windy Rocky Mountains, where the altitude ranges from about 7,000 to 10,000 feet. "The conditions in Colorado are different, of course, but they are just similar enough so that almost every species I've found there will grow here in the Northeast," he said.

Linked Material

Examples of linked material in this article can be found in paragraphs 8 and 9. Mr. Spain's background and the early years of his fascination with cacti are clustered in these two paragraphs.

Transitions

Transitions smooth the way for readers. The final sentence of paragraph 8 in "Cactuses" serves as a transition to the first sentence in paragraph 9:

> He began collecting cactuses around 1962 when he picked up
> a box of them at the Denver airport.
> "They turned out to fascinate me," he said.

Because of the transitional sentence, readers aren't in doubt as to who is speaking and why.

"Mapping" an Article

A good way to learn about the structure of any feature is to number the paragraphs on your second reading. Then, in a third reading, make a list of the paragraphs and the contents of each. You'll be making a "map" of the piece. The map will then be there to guide you as to how that particular writer delivered information to you.

For this map, I have noted the basic content of the paragraphs, the elements of the fictional devices used, and the other narrative techniques employed.

"Cactuses" has twelve paragraphs. Each is broken down into information about content, the function of the paragraph in the article, and how the information in the paragraph is delivered to the reader.

1. Lead + direct quote (direct observation; point of view; characterization)
2. Nut graf + direct quote (characterization)
3. Nut graf (2) + direct quote (plant information)
4. Setting (direct observation; description of Connecticut garden)
5. Plant information (summary)

6. Cultivation information + short quote (summary)
7. Cultivation information (summary)
8. Personal background of Mr. Spain (characterization)
9. Personal background + direct quote (characterization)
10. Outside corroboration #1 + quote (characterization)
11. Outside corroboration #2 + quote (characterization)
12. Plans + ending quote (characterization)

Where to Learn More

Feature stories are an art and a craft. Search for "feature story" or "feature article" in www.amazon.com to look at the number of excellent books that specifically address this form of nonfiction writing.

The Poynter Institute, a nonprofit organization devoted to the betterment of journalism, maintains a Web site that serves to teach and enlighten anyone with a passion for writing. See www.poynter.org. (Search the Poynter site for articles on feature stories, and don't miss Roy Peter Clark's columns at the same site.)

CHAPTER FOUR

Gardens Speak:
Sentences, Verbs, and Voice

The sentence. Two words into this chapter, I've already broken a rule. You know the definition of a sentence: You have been asked to define it since the third grade, perhaps before. A sentence has a subject (who or what is performing the action) and a verb (an action word, in the language of the lower grades); as you progressed in school, the verb with its qualifiers and complements was called a predicate, and you learned that a sentence states a complete thought. Then you learned that there are many kinds of sentences — simple, compound, complex, and so on.

You learned, too, from your teacher or professor's red-penciled diagnoses, about the maladies suffered by your sentences: incompleteness, over-subordination, subject–verb disagreement, redundancies, or the embarrassment of what in some quarters is called a comma splice (two sentences joined by an underweight comma). The business of English grammar seems as complex as neurosurgery.

If we gardeners, though, had to revisit and memorize the rules of grammar and punctuation and usage before we wrote about what we know, we'd want to rethink the idea. It's as if we had been asked as children to memorize the biomechanics of the body before learning to swim. Writers learn as they write. It's a never-ending journey.

Finding the Sentence in the Sentence (I)

William Miller, an eloquent arborist, was quoted by the fine writer Mac Griswold in an article in the *New York Times* on May 13, 1999, "Pruning With a Specialist's Touch." Mr. Miller described his pruning philosophy: "It's a matter of finding the tree in the tree."

Let's assume Mr. Miller is about to prune an overgrown Japanese maple. I take his comment to mean that he uses his trained arborist's eye to see in the untended shagginess the ideal shape the Japanese maple wants to be. A good arborist is also an artist.

People often need help in finding the sentence within the sentence. Reminders help: Straightforwardness is a virtue. Subjects appear in the beginning of sentences. Verbs follow. Then it's best to trim away everything that is extraneous to the meaning of the sentence.

Here's what I mean. I will repeat the conclusion of paragraph above:

> Then it's best to trim away everything that is extraneous to the meaning of the sentence.

A more economical way to say this:

> Trim away everything extraneous to the meaning of the sentence.

The phrase "then it's best" adds nothing to the meaning of the sentence, and can be misleading. The phrase is a matter of what is called *voice* — that is, the impression the reader gets of the personality of the writer. The phrase here, in a strict sense, does not serve the sentence.

The use of the word *that* in the original sentence ("that is extraneous") can be eliminated along with its verb *is*. (Now that I have brought up the subject of *that*, I urge you, for hundreds of reasons, including sorting out the judicious use of *that* and *which*, to acquire Bill Bryson's helpful and entertaining *Bryson's Dictionary of Troublesome Words: A Writer's Guide to Getting It Right*.)

Strengthening sentences may mean replacing a form of *to be* with precise, if not lively, verbs. In a first draft writers often string together disparate thoughts. *Is* and *are* serve a purpose. In the editing, however, the hunt begins for ways to strengthen sentences.

I suppose we could trim away the *away* after *trim*. The verb alone would suffice, but the sentence might be a bit terse. *Trim* in the context would seem to be self-explanatory, but then if you think about trimming a Christmas tree, the verb has an opposite meaning. Look carefully, at any rate, whenever you use words such as *away* and *up* with verbs. If you write "raise up your arms and grasp the branch, . . ." the word *up* is not needed. *Raise* implies an upward direction; it's fine by itself.

Finding the Sentence in the Sentence (II)

Take a look at this sentence:

> There weren't many farmstands in our area, and those that existed were located far apart and didn't have much to offer.

And this one:

> You had to drive a long way to find a farmstand in our area, and when you did find one, there wasn't much there, and then you had to drive miles to try to find another one.

Readers can wade into these garbled sentences to discover three problems with local farmstands. But the garden writer and editor Leslie Land solves this weighty word problem with elegance and clarity:

> Farmstands were few, far-between, and ill-stocked.

In my awkward sentences above Leslie Land's, I used several conventions often found in the work of beginning writers (and in the work of tired, experienced ones).

* *There* is a weak, imprecise sentence subject.
* *You* can be a weak and misleading sentence subject. (Writers directly addressing the reader must have a good reason for doing so.)
* *Area* is an overused and imprecise word. Avoid it if possible.
* The second sentence is unwieldy. Two sentences can be separated for clarity.

(Watch out for run-on sentences in your work. If you see two independent clauses linked by a comma — for example, "The botanical garden canceled the event, the hurricane threatened the day" — rewrite to correct.)

Verbs

The verb is the ringmaster of the sentence, the leader of the pack. In gardening, the "right plant, right place" advice usually pays a dividend; so does the writing advice "right noun, right verb."

Precise verbs can be tricky. The novelist F. Scott Fitzgerald wrote, "All fine prose is based on the verbs carrying the sentence." It's a good way to think of verbs, as carriers not only of the action of the sentence but also of the vitality of the entire thought.

We speak easily and naturally using *is, are, was,* and *were.* Replacing these words with more precise verbs results in stronger writing. (Practice this daily: Among the verbs you use in an e-mail correspondence, limit yourself to three forms of "to be".)

Dancing Verbs

Verlyn Klinkenborg, a writer who serves on the editorial board of the *New York Times,* is a master of verbs. His verbs sing, dance, fly, and soar off the page. So do his verbals, which are verbs used as other parts of speech (adjectives and adverbs and nouns).

The following sentences are taken from the lead paragraph of his profile, in the *New York Times Magazine,* of the plant explorer Dan Hinkley.

> The architecture of Dan Hinkley's garden on the Kitsap Peninsula in Washington State is native, shaped by old Douglas firs and a seeping bog. More than 50 kinds of arisaemas — called jack-in-the pulpit in North America — rocket from the soil. And one, Arisaema nepenthoides, stands fully erect, a single cobralike spathe beside a rotting stump crowned with ferns.

Let's look at the more interesting verbs and verbals:

- shaped
- seeping (verbal)
- rocket
- stands fully erect
- rotting (verbal)
- crowned

I often ask writing students to imagine what verbs they might have used in an early draft of Mr. Klinkenborg's description. I've asked myself this question too. What about those arisaemas rocketing from the soil? "Pushing up" comes to mind, or "emerging," or simply "coming up." But those arisaemas rocket, a different matter altogether. Even that stump is pumping out life, rotting yet crowned.

These sentences are so alive that the shaping, seeping, rocketing, erecting, rotting, and crowning are a symphony of action, so much, in fact, that even the phrase *cobralike spathe* (an adjective and a noun) won't be still — it zigzags, races, and pops off the page.

But beware as you look for unusual verbs. Making a verb of a noun or an adjective is a tricky business better left to the genius and artistry of a prose stylist such as John McPhee. (By the way, he employs two forms of the infinitive *to porpoise* to the delight of this reader in his latest book, *The Founding Fish*.)

Lay off dull verbs like *presents, forms,* and *implies.* Circle lively verbs as you read. Hoard them. You never know when you will want to dip into your stash.

Active vs. *Passive Voice*

Keep in mind the matter of the dreaded passive voice. You want your sentences to be lively — to show direct action. Consider this sentence:

> Three curving beds of daphne had been designed by the landscape architect to take advantage of the only full-sun spot on the south side of the house.

The sentence restated in active voice and with less clutter:

> The landscape architect designed three curving beds, planted with variegated daphne, for the full-sun spot on the south side of the house.

To test your sentence for active construction, try this analysis: Who/did what/to whom or what? Then make the "doer" the subject of an active verb. In this example, we find the subject of the sentence (who — landscape architect) followed by the verb (did what — designed) and a prepositional phrase (for what — full-sun spot). Why bother with active construction when it's just as easy to understand passive construction? Writers and readers want sentences with clarity, strength, and directness. Passive construction dilutes a sentence's effectiveness. Active verbs shine when they are on their own, unencumbered by auxiliary (helping) verbs such as *had been.* The verb *designed* is direct; *had been designed* takes the starch out of the action.

As for the clutter: The phrase *to take advantage of* is extra verbiage. We understand that the landscape architect is taking advantage of a full-sun spot. The word *only* is unnecessary. If there was more than one full-sun spot, the writer should have mentioned it. I've added the adjective *variegated* to describe the daphne for precision and clarity. After all, a landscape architect can design curving beds, but not the daphne.

Voice: Sound, Rhythm, and Tone

Now we come to the other "voice" that writers should heed. This "voice," in writing as in speech, has to do with sound and rhythm and tone. This voice is the sound of the writer's personality. Your naturalistic voice on the page is similar to the voice your friends hear when you tell a story.

Novice writers often pump out rather formal voices. Most of us try to sound more proper on the page than we do in conversation. Trapped into self-consciousness, it's as if our ninth-grade English teacher, Miss Priss, were sitting menacingly on one shoulder, waving her red pencil.

Practice will cure the curse of Miss Priss. It's a matter of unlearning. A natural, instinctive, and emotionally savvy voice lives within you, wanting to be free. (My own voice is loosened when writing a letter to a sympathetic friend. Give it a try.)

Pacing and timing in the text are important; you can slow down or speed up the reader. Follow long sentences with short ones or short ones with long ones. Rhythm can hypnotize readers. How can you tell what readers will hear? Read your work aloud at every stage. Read it aloud again, and again.

One way to cultivate your voice is to hear the voices of other writers. In fiction, read the short stories of Alice Munro. Read John McPhee. (His book *Oranges* is a masterpiece of narrative garden writing.) Read *The Orchid Thief,* by Susan Orlean. For these writers, voice is true to who they are. Read them and note the rhythm and variation of their sentences.

First, Second, or Third Person?

It's worth repeating these considerations, especially as you edit. Your decision as to point of view has to do with the general question of the intent of a piece. A writer may change her point of view in an article during its editing, or she may tone down the use of a first- or second-person pronoun.

A student wrote a skillful piece on garden-worthy salvias for one of my writing classes in the University of Connecticut Advanced Master Gardener Program. The story had verve as well as useful information. I liked it very much. (I happen to be a salvia nut anyway.)

But after I read her piece, I had to ask: On whose authority was this written? There were no quotations from anyone the writer had interviewed, no salvia experts cited from print sources.

The writer, as it turned out, was the expert. She had been a salvia-growing gardener for more than thirty years. But the writer kept this information to herself. The first-person pronoun is needed. The writer can easily solve this problem in the next draft.

We readers need to be told about the authority of the writer. However, once we are anchored in the knowledge and experience of the writer, a continued use of the first person is tedious. (I did this, and then I did that, and then I tried this . . .) Moderation is the key.

Exceptions in writing wriggle up as often as they do in life. Narrative travel writing and memoir writing often demand the first-person voice.

The use of the second person, *you,* can be tricky, very tricky, as I've mentioned. Avoid it unless you have a good reason for it.

The use of the first-person plural, *we,* can sound pretentious and at times condescending. Sometimes we can get away with it.

Third person refers to an omniscient narrator. Yet the choice of third person does not mean flirting with the deadening language of government, institutions, and corporations.

You don't want to sound like your bank. You do want to sound like yourself.

Listen to this third-person line, about orchids, from Susan Orlean in *The Orchid Thief:*

> They are at once architectural and fanciful and tough and dainty,
> a jewel of a flower on a haystack of a plant.

Readers don't need to see a first-person pronoun to understand there is a forceful personality behind it. Third person can be as lively and revealing as first.

Tricky Words/Tricky Language

In English, where the word *trim* can mean to cut away, to add to (as on a hat or a Christmas tree), to adjust sails to the direction of the wind, or to level off an airplane in flight, we poor practitioners of the language need help in navigation.

Buy a good, up-to-date, unabridged dictionary. Likewise a thesaurus.

The words *like* and *as* are not interchangeable. Many people misuse the word *hopefully.* This is where the witty and erudite Bill Bryson comes to the rescue *(Bryson's Dictionary of Troublesome Words).* What about *a while* and *awhile?* See *BDTW.*

On matters of form and style, writers and editors of newsletters, newspapers, and many magazines often depend on the *AP Stylebook,* published by the Associated Press. If you have any question about when to use the postal code for Arizona (AZ), or when to use the state's abbreviation (Ariz.), the *AP Stylebook* will clear up the matter.

Order the book in print or in an online version directly from the Associated Press, www.ap.org. (Caveat here: The *AP Stylebook* does not endorse the use of the serial comma, which the more erudite *Chicago Manual of Style,* 15th edition, does. Both books have grammar sections, by the way.)

Always good to have around are the classics: *The Elements of Style,* 4th edition, by William Strunk Jr. and E. B. White; and William Zinsser's *On Writing Well: An Informal Guide to Writing Nonfiction.* Many editors and writers recommend Claire Kehrwald Cook's *Line by Line: How to Edit Your Own Writing.*

Citing Botanical Names

Botanical names are cited by genus and species and, if appropriate, cultivar (a word culled from the phrase "cultivated variety"). The genus is capitalized and italicized; the species is written in lower case and italicized; the cultivar appears in single quotation marks and is not italicized. Sometimes the cultivar is capitalized, sometimes it appears in lower case.

An example: *Lamium orvala.* In an article for general readers, use the common name followed by the botanical name: Deadnettle *(Lamium orvala).*

In an article mentioning several plants in the same genus, abbreviate the genus name on second reference:

> *Lamium orvala*
> *L. maculatum* 'Album'
> *L. galeobdolon* 'Variegatum'

Hybrids (crosses between distinct species or genera) are noted with an ×: *Deutzia* × *elegantissima* 'Rosealind'.

The information above is the tip of the Linnaean iceberg, of course. I urge you to read the three-page section of the *American Horticulture Society Encyclopedia of Garden Plants* titled "Plant Origins and Names" if you aren't already familiar with the methods and history of plant classification.

But remember: Publications have style protocols. What you may think is the correct way to cite a botanical name may not fit in with a particular publication's policy. The *New York Times,* for example, does not usually print italicized words at all.

On Loving, and Writing about, Color

A garden writer referring to red flowers or fruits needs awakening. The rougy-silvery blush of a pomegranate is not the same as the orange-red of the persimmon.

And a writer using my personal bête noire, *colorful,* needs a remedial course in color theory.

I make up names of colors. It's great fun. (I'll never forget the fiction writer Sandra Cisneros describing, in an interview, the color of her new pickup truck: "menstruation red.") But I also consult a color wheel (you can buy one at any art store for a few dollars) and look at lists of colors in books about color.

I recommend the book *The Colorist,* by Shigenobu Kobayashi, which designates 130 color names. The book's system is derived from the Nippon Color & Design Research Institute's "Design Tone 130." Other books use other systems. The purpose of looking at colors and the names of colors is to broaden our ideas about color and to make our writing more lively and precise.

People often use the words *tint, tone,* and *shade* interchangeably, and *tint,* especially, as a synonym for *color.* Here's the scoop.

- *hue:* the pure color
- *value:* the relative lightness or darkness of a color
- *tint:* a hue with white added
- *tone:* a hue with gray added
- *shade:* a hue with black added

Whatever the color, it isn't colorful. We can assume it (the plant, the sky, the perennial bed) is full of color. It's up to you to tell us *what* color.

CHAPTER FIVE

The Traveling Gardener:
Observing and Writing about Place

Travel writing. Here's the spine of the idea: The writer has, in her own person, traveled to a garden—perhaps an estate or other public garden. She wants to write about it for her gardening club newsletter or local newspaper.

As I write on a clear, bright Sunday morning in July, the travel section of the *New York Times* is nearby, tempting me from my writing tasks.

I will discuss this section with you briefly not because you want to become a travel writer; I know you are interested in gardens. I'm suggesting that we take a look at the ways you can project that interest into the world through the travel story.

Journalistic travel writing is about information: It includes where to go and what to do when you are there. Articles are often celebratory or cautionary, sometimes both. A travel section is shaped by the editor's vision. Articles are restricted by word count and topical elements. Readers use these stories as they would a guidebook.

The subjects of the articles in today's *New York Times* Travel Section include: philosophy and architecture (Heidelberg, Ludwigsburg); adventure on a remote, ancient site (a single island in the Outer Hebrides); fossil hunting (Jurassic Coast of England); and bird watching (Hawk Mountain, Pennsylvania).

These stories reflect the direct experience of the writers and are written in the first person. They are finished off with a sidebar of practical information: how to get there, where to stay, where to eat, and roughly what it will all cost.

A traveling gardener would slant her story toward other aspects of Heidelberg, for example. She would write about the things that would interest a gardener: public gardens, arboreta, botanical gardens, landscaping around the city's ancient university, horticultural or agricultural festivals, summer window boxes, private gardens, garden tours, or perhaps a signature flower, tree, or woody shrub of the city.

At the end of today's section, there is still another example of nonfiction writing, the personal essay. Gillian Tindall writes about a little-known and recently built (2001) First World War memorial at a newly planted arboretum near Birmingham, England. She was deeply moved by the Shot at Dawn Memorial to more than three hundred young British soldiers who were executed by their fellows for "desertion in the face of the enemy." In her short essay, the writer reflects on the almost-century-long secrecy shrouding these executions.

It's a lesson to us traveling gardeners to keep our eyes and ears open, and to be, in Joan Didion's famous admonition to writers, "a person on whom nothing is lost."

But like everything else in life and in writing, the nuanced variations of travel writing are as complex as the universe of individual experience, sensibility, intent, talent, and craft.

A garden-related travel story can be as basic as a list of places to visit in San Francisco repeating the obvious, such as a walk through Golden Gate Park. Yet you never know what you might see in this world-famous park to make it new to your readers.

Opportunities to write about travel and gardens are almost limitless. The urge to make gardens of whatever definition seems to be an inbred human impulse; to make a garden is an act of culture. Gardeners learn by doing, of course, but also by seeing. This is where travel writing comes in.

Let's say you travel to the Berkshires, to Lenox, Massachusetts. You visit Naumkeag, the Choate family estate, where the influential American landscape architect Fletcher Steele worked on its stunning gardens for three decades, until the mid-twentieth century. You might consider the following subjects to fold into an article on Naumkeag:

- Analysis of Fletcher Steele's design for Naumkeag decade by decade
- Fletcher Steele's influence on American landscape design
- Naumkeag's influence on American landscape design
- Preservation of Fletcher Steele's design at Naumkeag
- Costs of preservation and renovation of Naumkeag's gardens
- Influence of Asian travel on Mabel Choate and the gardens
- Native American culture in western Massachusetts and its influence on farming practices at Naumkeag
- Farming in the Berkshires in the nineteenth and twentieth centuries and at Naumkeag
- Planting of annuals at Naumkeag
- Invasive plants at Naumkeag
- Aboriculture at Naumkeag
- Use of stones at Naumkeag
- Geology of the Berkshires
- Bird watching at Naumkeag
- Influence of Moorish landscape architecture on Fletcher Steele and Naumkeag
- Influence of Art Deco on Fletcher Steele
- Visiting the major estate gardens of Lenox
- Mabel and Fletcher: the relationship that built a garden

The ways to look at Naumkeag are limited only by the imagination. The traveling gardener must keep open her eyes, ears, heart, and mind.

Travel writing provides a story, a narrative map to a place. A travel piece for a newspaper or magazine will most likely include information almost as specific as a directional map: You will enter the garden on its northeast side, off Angelita Road, beyond the willow-fringed, egg-shaped pond.

❧

Literary travel writing is multilayered with meaning and context and character. The British writer Lawrence Durrell's nonfiction books about living in a particular place in the Mediterranean are a fine example of the genre. His books are driven by a need not to inform the reader of the basics necessary to make the trip, but rather to bring the experience to life on the page with the eye of the novelist he is.

Durrell dives deep in *Bitter Lemons*. He has moved to Cyprus immediately after the Second World War. The island is so thoroughly and lovingly rendered with such broad historical and sociological perspective that it becomes a character in itself. Durrell's narratives are character-driven, whether the character is a place or a person.

The best travel writing is the admixture of direct experience, observation, character analysis, history, geology, anthropology — you name it, if it has to do with human beings and their interaction with place.

How you are to write about place depends on your interests, your nature as a person and a writer, and the intent of the piece you want to write.

✒

What I understand to be the heart of writing about place (and that includes gardens) came to me the year I turned thirty and traveled to Egypt. I remember the moment in Luxor when I shifted from tourist to traveler.

I rose before dawn, left the hotel, and walked the short distance to Luxor Temple in the dark cool desert air. A seated statue of the Eighteenth Dynasty pharaoh Amenhotep II had intrigued me the previous day; I wanted to see him again, without the chattering of the tour group or guide.

I hadn't expected to find the temple guardians on the ground at their morning prayers among the forlorn, ruined stones of this great civilization. It was clear that they slept among the stones. I made my way to Amenhotep. A temple guardian followed me in the smoke gray light. Bit by bit, the light of the sweet pink-grapefruit dawn brought the ancient pharaoh's wisdom to life. I saw the unchanging equanimity of this great king, three thousand years deceased. The twentieth-century young American woman disappeared; the guardian and the pharaoh were present in the dawn as they had been for centuries.

This and other moments on this trip called me to write about place. I wanted to tell the story of my trip to Egypt, but hadn't any idea how to go about it. That would come after a long apprenticeship. But now I realize that unless I've written about a place I've visited, I don't really understand what I've seen, or what it might mean.

More than two decades after my trip to Egypt, I read Lawrence Durrell's 1960 essay on place called "Landscape and Character." I offer his advice to you because I know it is the truth from my own years of looking and traveling and writing. He writes:

> The great thing is to try and travel with the eyes of the spirit wide open, and not too much factual information. To tune in, without reference, idly — but with real inward attention. It is to be had for the feeling, that mysterious sense of rapport, of identity with the ground. You can extract the essence of a place once you know how. If you just get still as a needle you'll be there.

"Still as a needle." To be quiet and still is an art and a very individual matter. For some, stillness is an innate quality; for others, it must be cultivated. Yet gardeners know stillness and focus. It's difficult to imagine tending a garden without these qualities of attention.

On the practical side, I can suggest a few things that may be of help in cultivating that "sense of rapport, of identity with the ground." You may not need them at all, or they may not fit your way of being in the world. I can only tell you what has evolved in my own writing life over two decades. It's a way of keeping a "beginner's mind," as the phrase is used in Zen Buddhism; there are ways to scuttle your preconceptions.

- Visit a garden by yourself (you can set your own pace and avoid distractions).
- Visit early in the day or late in the afternoon (when the light is soft).
- Know only the bare basics about the place you are visiting (you can research everything later). Otherwise, your mind might be set about what you are about to see and you will miss the freshness and newness of the experience.
- Take a minimum of notes. (I used to try to write down everything, meaning I missed the experience of being present.)
- Take a minimum of photographs, perhaps just as you are ready to leave.
- If you are to interview someone at the garden, arrive at least forty-five minutes

early so you can breathe in the place on your own. (If it's a private garden, ask permission, of course.)

- Listen.
- Smell.
- Taste.

Resources for the Traveling Gardener

When you are ready to research, consider the following resources for information:

- ❧ The publicity or public relations department of the garden
- ❧ Local chamber of commerce
- ❧ Convention and Visitors Bureau
- ❧ Guidebooks
- ❧ Online article search

Do your best to write from a fresh angle, especially about famous gardens. Use your own sensibility to find something other writers have missed. Major public gardens often employ historians, who are excellent people to interview. See what you can uncover.

TWO EXAMPLES

The first is a brief travel news story, one in which I wanted to convey a matter of interest to garden lovers.

New Book for Lovers of Fletcher Steele's Gardens

For many lovers of American gardens, the landscape architect Fletcher Steele is their Gershwin and the famous Blue Steps at Naumkeag are his rhapsody. Happily, the landscape historian Robin Karson's 1989 fascinating and out-of-print book, *Fletcher Steele, Landscape Architect: An Account of the Gardenmaker's Life, 1885–1971,* is available in a revised and handsome paperbound edition (LALH/University of Massachusetts Press, 2003, $34.95). The new book has 50 additional images of Steele's work at Naumkeag and other estates, many in color. Karson first learned of Steele after a visit to Naumkeag in Stockbridge, Mass., in 1983; Steele had worked on Naumkeag from the 1930s until 1958, when his wealthy patron, Mabel Choate, died. Miss Choate left the house and gardens to the Trustees of Reservations, which opens the estate to the public annually from Memorial Day weekend to Columbus Day. (The Blue Steps are on the cover of the book; you can see them for yourself for an $8 fee from 10 a.m. until 5 p.m. daily in season. 5 Prospect Hill Road, Stockbridge, Mass., 413-298-3239; www.thetrustees.org.)

Why is "New Book" a news story? It's short. It's to the point. It answers the questions of journalism: who, what, where, when, and how. The story conveys to the reader basic information about a new book.

Yet there are two elements in these 170-plus words that make it a particular kind of news story.

1. *The soft lead.* The first sentence, the hook or lead of the story, is called a soft lead. A "hard" lead might be as follows: "The landscape historian Robin Karson has published the second edition of . . ." I decided to write a softer lead. Which to choose? The decision depends on the intent and the preference of the publication. Yet the subject matter often dictates a choice for a hard or a soft lead. If you were a reporter for your local newspaper, and you were covering a fire in a neighborhood home, a hard-news lead is more appropriate. The subject matter has immediacy and is newsworthy for its own sake. A story about a fire has its own push. It is a hard-news story. The reader doesn't need to be hooked in.

2. *The ending.* Hard-news stories don't end in an invitation to the reader to take action of any kind. The story above, about Robin Karson's new book, is a short travel-related piece. The story would never belong in the hard-news section of a newspaper or news magazine. It would, however, fit in the news section of a gardening magazine, in the house and garden section of a newspaper, or, as it was conceived, as a short piece in a newspaper's travel section.

The second example is the following story I wrote for the *New York Times* (published November 5, 2000) about a hiking trip I took to Zion National Park. I hadn't any intention to write about it, but I fell in love with the geology and the plants and the place. The article is a bit unusual in the travel-writing genre (at least for one aimed at a general audience) in that the plants are a part of the adventure.

I also understood that there was some hard news here. The shuttle service running through the heart of the canyon was only a week old at the time of my visit. Banning cars in the canyon was big news after a century of automobile traffic. (See chapter 8 for the query letter I wrote to the *Times* making the case for this article.)

For many publications, a travel article is written in such a way that the reader can follow in the footsteps of the writer.

When I went to Zion, I kept a news and entertainment blackout. I didn't read a magazine or newspaper or turn on a radio or television, and I cut down phone communication to almost zero. It was my way of staying "still as a needle." I did read about Zion when I was there, but not before. (No trip to Utah should be undertaken without reading Edward Abbey's *Desert Solitaire* and Wallace Stegner's *Mormon Country;* likewise, *Wildflowers of Zion National Park,* by Dr. Stanley L. Welsh, and *Shrubs and Trees of the Southwest Uplands,* by Francis H. Elmore.)

This article was followed by a detailed sidebar of practical information for the traveler. (You can read it online at www.nyt.com at no cost.)

Canyon of Colorful Surprises

When a high-country craving comes over me like a thunderclap, there's nothing to be done except pack up. Last June, struck by my annual hunger for great walls of rock, dry heat, Fremont cottonwoods, darting lizards and a bit of water flashing silver in the sun, I decided to go hiking in southwestern Utah on my own.

Seven days in Zion National Park. The trip opened before me as if I had consulted an oracle. Zion Canyon, just a piece of the 229-square-mile park, turned out to be the most beautiful pink, buff, dusty red, veiled green and emerald rock garden in the world. I had the luck to meet companionable trail mates, and my hike into the Zion Narrows, with its sheer sandstone cliffs and so-called hanging gardens, went far beyond my expectations. And a bonus was the National Park Service's high-season ban on private vehicles in Zion Canyon.

"No more cars in national parks," the writer and passionate desert lover Edward Abbey thundered more than 30 years ago. Walk, he said, "or ride horses, bicycles, mules, wild pigs — anything" but motor vehicles. I doubt the prickly spirit of Cactus Ed is soothed by the bright new fleet of propane-fueled buses that operate from early April through October, but it is a serious attempt by the National Park Service, begun in May, to balance the perennial tension between public access and conservation.

So I rode the 14.6-mile Canyon shuttle loop early and late, up- and down-canyon, as they say at Zion. One day, I even walked a few miles along the road, breathing deeply, not missing the 5,000 cars that once spewed fumes here daily in the summer heat. I wondered how soon I could return, first in autumn to see big-toothed maples flashing scarlet, and again in spring when the tiny lavender and white Zion shooting star awakens and rockets from secret wet places.

From Las Vegas, Zion National Park is a nearly three-hour northeasterly drive, a useful introduction to the park itself. Like a court jester, the land masks and unmasks itself along the way. Flat desert gives way to the spot where the Colorado Plateau — that uplifted lima-bean-shaped land that rises in parts of Utah, Colorado, Arizona and New Mexico — cozies up to the mountains and valleys of the Great Basin.

Just past St. George, Utah, I turned off I-15 onto State Route 9 toward the town of Hurricane (pronounced there far more softly and more quickly than is usual: HUR-ah-kun). The limestone Hurricane Cliffs, the western boundary of the Markagunt

Plateau, opens up, and its layered deep wine, chocolate and white rock was softly bronzed and alive in the light of a summer's evening.

As these flat-topped tablelands were lifted up and up, the Virgin River cut through them. A tributary of the Colorado, the Virgin is the traveler's companion on I-15, starting in Arizona's northwest corner. Just before the Utah border, the cleft of Black Rock Canyon offers a preview of the dramatic topography to come. The Virgin's north fork is responsible for Zion Canyon, razoring its way through the Markagunt Plateau to make possible this journey into the white and vermilion lands of the Mesozoic era.

I'd chosen a motel in Springdale, Zion's gateway town (winter population, 350), for the length of its swimming pool and its proximity to the park. The motel, the Cliffrose Lodge, was a five-minute walk from the South Entrance, and my room overlooked at least three acres of lush gardens, where I marveled over the likes of a weeping blue atlas cedar, a Japanese maple called sango kaku and a gorgeous blue globed spruce.

On my first day, after mapping out a hiking plan for the week, I walked to the park and took a shuttle bus to the Zion Lodge stop. I walked across the road to the head of the Emerald Pools Trail, a moderate two-mile loop (part of which is paved). My reward was three small basins, carved into the rock ledges by flowing water.

There, it is possible to see one of the great delights of Zion: evidence of multiple life zones chasing each other around the park, playing hide-and-seek with soil, climate, exposure, light, elevation. Prickly pear cavorts with cottonwood, and a turn on a trail may quickly reveal a surprising microclimate, as it does at the lower pool here, where Heaps Canyon Creek tumbles off a cantilevered rocky ledge. The day was hot, the damp shade cool.

Navajo sandstone is the prevalent structural material of Zion, and in this wet alcove carved into a side canyon I took a good look at what I came to think of as not columbine, but Columbine, its platonic ideal. This was golden columbine, Aquilegia chrysantha (as I discovered later), a dwarf of the species. A few plants grew here and there, straight from the sandstone, or so it appeared. Buttercup yellow with tall spurs (well, tall for a two-inch flower), I would see them again and again by trickles of water, in seeps, and in the hanging gardens all through the canyon. The vast Zion rock garden can set off a tiny plant as if it were a jewel.

By early the next morning, I had a couple of other walks under my belt, and I was barreling up the rocky, desertlike Hidden Canyon Trail. This was a hike, not a walk, along a two-mile switchbacked trail, an 850-foot ascent. Just as I was thinking how very fine all this was, the trail curved to the right and hugged a wall to which a chain was attached. A deep drop-off seemed just below my right shoulder.

My palms dampened. I sat down to give myself a talking-to. Surely I could overcome this bit of acrophobia. Two hikers passed. One looked back to ask, "Are you all right?"

I made a good decision to confess instead of trying to save face, for in this manner, I met Ole Tom and Ole Gus, as they invariably referred to each other. Tom kindly offered to turn around and let me follow him up to the mouth of Hidden Canyon, which hangs 800 feet above the floor of Zion Canyon. I did. It wasn't far. I managed by keeping my eyes on the heels of Tom's boots instead of the chasm to my right.

We rejoined Gus on the trail, and in the brief time it took us to hike back to the bottom, we had sketched out the basics, in the manner of hiking trail acquaintances. Tom and Gus were teachers from Florida, on a monthlong 8,000-mile driving and hiking trip through the West. Because I was lucky enough to meet them (and they are both slightly more into middle age than myself), I hiked farther, longer and higher in the three days we walked and climbed together than I would have by myself.

Hidden Canyon was only their warm-up, and they invited me to accompany them on a hike into the Narrows, farther up Zion Canyon, that afternoon. I accepted, and hoped they wouldn't talk too much. (They were probably hoping the same thing.)

Zion Canyon is 200 yards wide at the Temple of Sinawava (a Paiute god), the northernmost shuttle stop. Riverside Walk, the gateway trail to the Narrows, begins here, and continues for a mile to the trail's end. There, those who are equipped with a good walking stick and proper footwear plunge into the river for day hikes of varying lengths. (Most of this trail is through the river itself, though the river can be skirted in certain places on its banks.)

We chose to hike the Narrows to Orderville Canyon, about three miles. Hikers wanting to walk the entire 16-mile length of the Narrows can do so in two ways: an overnight trip, or a strenuous 12-hour hike. Both begin at Chamberlain's Ranch, about a 90-minute drive from Zion Canyon, near the park's northeast corner. Either way, the hike requires a backcountry permit ($5), and much planning and preparation.

On the hot, dry afternoon we headed for the Narrows, the river seemed to call. The lovely Riverside Walk reeled by, a blur of green. Tom and Gus were just as focused. No chitchat. We stepped into the river.

I immediately understood the park service's admonition against hiking there alone. The river was deeper and swifter than I had expected, but far more beautiful. As the roughly 1,600-foot-high sandstone walls (among the world's highest such cliffs) narrowed and the river moved us forward, I thought, these aren't the bowels of the Earth, but its womb.

One foot must follow another carefully in the river, through moving water, over small rocks, over ledges, over moss; the walking stick taps out safe passage. The chilly water, welcome on this hot day, was mid-thigh for me, almost waist-high in deeper places. Ledges in the great walls and along the river bank of this perfect rock garden are home to velvet ash and box elder, netleaf hackberry and, on oddly sheltered sites here and there, the occasional white fir, escaped from the ridges above.

Set at the margins of the river bank and in the fine compositions of hanging gardens, the smaller plants of the Narrows showcase the splendid gardening hand of nature. Maidenhair fern, horsetail, Jones reedgrass, and bright buttery columbine play against reddish terra-cotta walls deepening to burgundy as we walked into the gathering shadow of late afternoon.

Tom and Gus and I determined our course of crossings and wadings. We exchanged only snippets of conversation as the walls of the canyon enclosed us more and more, its high ridges like a scalloped shell above us. We perched on a slice of sandstone beneath a cliff and ate small green apples. A gaggle of nearly naked French tourists shouted and shrieked as they darted past us, their rubber sandals slapping in the water.

The river was shallower as we approached the closed-in arms of Orderville Canyon to our right. We'd been hiking for only two miles or so in the water, but we were in another realm. A short distance ahead, the walls of the Narrows closed to about 30 feet. Above, the upper world was a slot of soft light. Around us was tawny twilight. Gus and I turned right and entered the cavelike Orderville Canyon.

Soon, the men were ready to turn around, although I thought perhaps we could have walked another half-mile before we were in danger of losing the light on the way back. I didn't want to leave, but I did. Along the way, I saw five honey-colored husks fastened hard to the sandstone walls, shucked off by locustlike insects already on their way to whatever comes next.

Although it was early evening, the sky brightened as we made our way through the widening canyon toward dry land. Hungry, yet well satisfied, we walked out of the river and the place where we had glimpsed the warm sandstone heart of the West.

About "Canyon"

I suggest, if you are interested in visiting public or private gardens (or landscapes), that you take a look at "Canyon" from the point of view of its structure.

The lead of the story reveals why I traveled to Zion; the nut graf grounds the story into the reality of the place and the hard-news angle: the ban on cars and the shuttle service.

Zion National Park has been part of the National Park Service for a century or more — why would the Travel Section of the *New York Times* be interested in yet another story about this well-known site? The hard news about the shuttle made all the difference.

The article is personal. It is written in the first person. The story is about what I saw and experienced, and organized around the core idea that the reader can follow in the writer's footsteps.

Read the article again. Number the paragraphs. Make a list of the kinds of information contained within each. Personal observation? Historical background? Geologic facts? Current information?

Any article you read is an opportunity to look at structure and learn from it to move forward your own writing.

❦

Writing about place is a way of being in love with the world. It's an important motivation for many writers, one that cuts to the bone. No writer has a better opportunity for being in love with the world than one who writes about gardens and plants.

Fortunately, in writing, meaning still counts. Writers want to tell people about what they've seen. They want to read about what others have seen. We profess in this profession. This reading and writing deepens our experience of the world.

Telling Stories

All gardens are a form of autobiography.

—Robert Dash

26 October 2004

Dear Reader,

Jessica Mitford — the English writer and journalist who in 1965 lifted the lid on the questionable practices of the funeral industry in *The American Way of Death* — once revealed what she did when, swamped by information, she couldn't find her way into a piece of writing. She wrote a letter to a friend.

Mitford's friendly and direct voice on the page is with me still. In 1977, I heard her speak at the San Francisco Press Club. She had a piercing upper-class English accent (she was one of the fabulous Mitford sisters, after all) and a fierce look about her eyes.

Jessica Mitford lived with her American husband across the Bay from San Francisco, in Oakland, and they were famously and furiously left wing. Journalists at the *San Francisco Chronicle* loved to quote her: She was spicy, drop-dead witty, unerring in her aim.

She was called Decca by those who knew her. I got this from reading the *Chron,* but it sticks with me because she spoke to her readers as friends.

It wasn't a political diatribe she delivered on November 6, 1977. She spoke about how she suddenly became a writer.

Her husband, for business reasons, had set about to study the business of funerals. That was how Mitford learned that America's bereaved were deceived, duped, and left debt-ridden.

She wrote an article salted with her outrage. She sent it to a magazine called *Westways,* and was stunned at its acceptance. She had not considered herself a writer (though her sister Nancy was among the most celebrated of her generation); instead, she had always thought of herself as "virtually unemployable."

This phrase galvanized me. It suggested there was a life to be lived after thirty. I was sitting in this audience dressed in my only good outfit, a black velvet blazer, wine-red silky blouse, and charcoal gray straight wool skirt. I had quit my job as a junior high teacher a year before, withdrawn the contents of my meager pension, and taken off for Egypt. Now I was back in San Francisco. What was next?

I hit the pavement applying for jobs in companies ranging from advertising agencies to a giant food provider, but the pavement hit back. (Virtually unemployable, I thought.)

I studied how to be an interviewee. I memorized *What Color Is Your Parachute?* But I was far more interested in the people behind those desks than in their companies. (What were they thinking? Who were they really?) Could I be a successful shill of institutional food? Unlikely. I preferred laboring alone in my kitchen with *Couscous and Other Good Food from Morocco.*

Meanwhile, I was tending a hundred houseplants in my small apartment while the couscous plumped. I dreamed about writing something about Egypt. But I had never known a writer, except a woman in my yoga class. She seemed to be a goddess. Her life had nothing to do with mine.

I would wait a long time before a satisfying solution presented itself. On one side of the idea would be my life. The other side would look something like this: people + plants + writing.

With affection,
Paula P.

Why Write a Letter to Readers?

I felt stuck. I wanted to show you two things: first, one version of the story of how becoming a writer slowly worked its way into my mind; second, what you can do when overwhelmed by information. Writing this letter seemed to clear the palate, the way a tart lemon sorbet might do between a rich first course and an intensely flavored second.

But if you are to tell a story, it's important to make a distinction. Did the story you want to tell actually happen? Because of the form I used above, a letter addressing readers, I think you assume I was telling a true story. I was. But it is worth a reminder here of the difference between fiction and nonfiction.

Clarify Intent: Fact or Fiction?

Over the years I've met people in professions other than writing who have said they were "writing stories." When I ask what sort of stories, whether short stories (fiction) or essays (nonfiction), I often hear, "Oh, I don't know; they're just stories."

But there is a difference, and an important one. Let's say there are two pieces of writing in front of you. They have the following elements in common:

- First-person point of view ("I")
- Length
- Scenes
- Dialogue
- Character development
- Closely observed detail
- Narrative arc

The difference is this: When the writer uses the first person in a short story or a novel, she is constructing a character whose main purpose is to serve the story — that is, the plot, made up of action and theme. In fiction, a first-person narrator is a point-of-view character, constructed by the writer. (Point-of-view characters are written in the third person, and in a number of variations on both first and third, and, more rarely, second.) The job of this narrator is to deliver the story, to move the action and theme forward. Most works of fiction are exercises of the imagination. Even those that are based on the author's experience are also exercises of the imagination.

A work of fiction does not claim to be the objective truth. A fiction writer is trying to create an effect—that is, a feeling—that has its own truth, but it is not the truth of a writer of nonfiction.

In nonfiction, the first-person narrator has another job. Here the narrator is in the service of truth. In general nonfiction, the narration is based on impeccable research and reporting.

Within the subset of nonfiction called the personal narrative (the personal essay, memoir, or autobiography), the writer is not only expected to be truth-telling but is also expected to dig deep into her mind and heart. She is a researcher and reporter of her own life, but she is looking for emotional truth, her own truth. The goal in the personal narrative is to find and express that truth and to engage understanding and wisdom.

Deepen Your Nonfiction Story

Let's say you want to write about your grandmother and her garden. You want to write about your memories of this grandmother, and what was in her garden, and what it was like standing in the hot sun and eating tomatoes in August straight from the vine.

An essay (I use "essay," "personal writing," and "personal narrative" interchangeably) on this subject can take shape in many ways. A person may write, "I remember my grandmother's garden . . ." and explore no further than its tender green beans and the heft of the grandmother's trowel.

But life is complex. Good writing, along with the truth, requires us to be willing to explore deeply. A grandmother may have survived a labor camp in World War II; was widowed at thirty; or never learned to read. The story complicates itself, as all life does. When you are writing about a garden from memory, think about what Robert Dash, a wildly inventive artist and gardener, said: "All gardens are a form of autobiography." If this is so, then the world of a garden can open up for someone writing a personal narrative. What did her garden say about your grandmother? This will be your speculation, of course, but your speculation will be grounded in what you know to be true.

The tone, as well as the subject, of a personal essay can embrace the full range of human experience. There is no limit to kind of subject, thought, or feeling that can be invoked by engaging this simple six-letter word on a page: *garden.*

Consider the fine book *The Writer in the Garden,* edited by Jane Garmey. In it, you can read writers from Homer to Michael Pollan on the subjects of gardens and plants. You'll hear voices from the droll (Vita Sackville-West and Gertrude Jekyll), to the lyrical and polemic (W. S. Merwin), to the clever with astonishing subtexts (M. F. K. Fisher and Cynthia Kling).

Identify Subtext or Theme

The best personal narratives set out to dislodge conventional thinking and self-delusion. William Hazlitt, an eighteenth-century English writer, wrote an essay entitled "On the Pleasures of Hating." I'd like to see a contemporary essayist follow up with "On the Pleasures of Hating Gardens." It may turn out that the essayist really hates herself for her slovenly, neglectful, and even occasional mean-spirited attitude toward her garden. Or maybe not.

The theme of a personal narrative is critical. Sometimes a writer doesn't know what the theme will be as she writes. It reveals itself much later. So what is a subtext or a theme? It's what's really on your mind. You may be writing about the apples you remember on your neighbor's tree. But when all is said and done, your piece may be about how afraid you were to leave home. The apples seem to be the subject of your piece, but the subtext is your fear.

Allowing the subtext to emerge is one of the great rewards of this lonely and often frustrating endeavor, writing. You may very well find out what is really on your mind, even if you have only an inkling, a hunch, a wisp of an idea before you get going. All writing, good writing, has purpose and intent.

And the lovely thing about this task of writing is its evolutionary nature. A garden may be a form of autobiography, but it's a constantly changing story. So is your writing.

EXAMPLE

The following is an essay by my colleague Maryann Macdonald. She has written two dozen books, short stories, and essays. "Gardening Shoes I Have Known" is an example of what a wise teacher of mine, Vivian Gornick, might call a "memoir-ish essay."

Although it is ostensibly about the shoes the writer has worn while gardening, the story incorporates a theme. In Maryann Macdonald's memoir-ish essay, she guides us over not a year in her life, but instead the years of her gardening life. This is the temporal arc of her story. This is what ties it to the genre of writing known as a memoir, which is a book-length first-person narrative that illuminates a specified time of the writer's life.

Gardening Shoes I Have Known

The concept of having shoes just for gardening never occurred to me before I lived in England. In the backyard of my childhood family home in the western suburbs of Detroit, I suppose I wore Keds when I planted that pussy willow tree beside the garage, or perhaps my brown school shoes when I weeded dandelions out of the clay soil surrounding my tomato plants and carrot seedlings. My Keds were navy blue. My mother wouldn't let us have white Keds . . . too difficult to clean. Apart from these, all I owned were my Sunday patent-leather pumps and maybe a pair of slipper socks. There were shoes for school, playing in, and church/parties — that was it. Life was simple. You ate your raspberries right off the bush.

I didn't plant or tend a garden during my teenage years. I was too busy trying to be cool, wearing black needle-toed boots and white stilettos. These suited neither my personality nor my gardening hobby, and they didn't last long. By my early twenties, I was planting melons and pumpkins in the backyard of the Archie Bunker–style clapboard house where I lived in Washington, D.C. I suspect I planted them barefoot, with marigolds as a natural insecticide around the perimeter of the patch. Washington summers were hot. Leisure shoes had not yet been invented. I came home from work, kicked off my shoes, and padded around in my L'Eggs panty hose, more often than not putting holes in them. But if I did garden in shoes, it was probably in flip-flops or whatever shoes I happened to have worn to work that day.

The two pairs I remember most vividly are green woven straw slingbacks and camel leather platform sandals with straps that twined around my ankles like affectionate snakes. I never thought about ruining my shoes back then. I just wore them out and pitched them for the next style coming up the pike. Besides, the crabgrass underfoot was dry. I had no flower beds, only azalea bushes. I watered these and my melons and never gave a thought to spatters on my shoes.

My gardens in England were different. I guess you could say they were my first grown-up gardens. I acquired the first when I was thirty-two. It was L-shaped, surrounded by nine apple trees and one plum, with daffodils poking out of the grass in the springtime. I had children by this time, and a sandbox and a play-house my husband built himself. I was learning to cook properly, and planted sage and rosemary and a bay tree. I was out in this garden a lot, trying to dig up the beds, which hadn't been manured in years. I needed strong boots to push the prongs of the steel pitchfork into the earth. I tried my hiking boots, but these got clumps of mud stuck in the treads. I bought a pair of Wellingtons, because it rained a lot and the garden was often muddy. But they were bulky and hot in summer and cold in winter.

I ended up settling for a pair of green Swedish wooden clogs, painted with lilies of the valley, that I had bought on the Boulevard St. Germaine, when my elder child was a baby and I lived in Paris, and had no garden. I ruined the clogs planting a broom bush, pinks, scattering forget-me-not seeds after the flowers had blossomed, and cutting back pyracantha and lavender. We moved out of that house after six years, leaving the paddling pool and my children's childhood behind. But by then I knew a lot more about gardening and had discovered better shoes for it.

My next London garden was Victorian, a long, narrow one with a summer house at the end of it, a shady right side with a pear tree and a perennial bed on the other. It was walled and neglected, like the Secret Garden. I loved it and hated it at the same time. I knew it would go nowhere I didn't take it, and I was busy raising a family and writing children's books. The soil was impoverished, the roses diseased. My daughters danced around the lawn in their pink ballet shoes, picking flowers. I wanted to do the same.

Instead, I bought a pair of plastic buckle-on platform shoes with nails embedded in the soles. I used these to pace the lawn, to aerate the soil. My footsteps stuck in the heavy earth and I could barely trudge ahead. I dragged out the hiking boots again and lashed the spikes tighter. I aerated that damn lawn.

About this time, Minnetonka moccasins were making a comeback. My mother bought me a pair for my fortieth birthday at Harry's Army Surplus on Telegraph Road near her home in Michigan. They were tan and had rubber soles, along with the traditional fake Indian beading. These were just about perfect for my gardening and my life.

They were tough and attractive enough to be worn all day, gardening being an interruptible pastime. They prevented many a pair of good canvas espadrilles from being destroyed by sudden impulses to plant, water, clip and dig. I wore the mocs with flowered Kenzo jeans (anyone remember those?) and a pink sweatshirt. This I remember as my garden birthing outfit. In it, I tore down the diseased roses and planted wisteria, pruned back the lilacs, trained clematis and Virginia creeper up the brick walls.

I whacked that border into shape, planting aquilegia and iris. I planned a basketball court, and then turned it into a terrace. In short, I made that garden into what it was meant to be. Only one thing nagged at me . . . it lacked a water feature.

With my best friend and fellow garden shopper I drove out to the Enfield Water Garden Centre one spring. We were looking for a fountain, and we found one: an Italian marble wall fountain that could be lugged away for only five hundred English pounds. Reader, I bought it, and then guess what I found?

The PERFECT gardening shoes! Hard green rubber soles, soft green rubber cloggy tops, lined with comfy flannel, made in fashionable France, no less. They were totally strong, waterproof and didn't even look bad. I got the fountain delivered and installed. My garden, for one lovely summer, was perfect. I watered and dead-headed in a trance, scarcely able to believe it was mine. Then we decided to move.

Now in my fifties, I live in an apartment in New York City. It's a fourth-floor walkup. It has a neglected roof terrace. My landlord, a friend, has asked me to do something with it. I'm gearing up. I signed up for a class at the Horticultural Society on rooftop and terrace design. I'm thinking greenhouse. I'm thinking pergola. My shoes are waiting by the door. But there will be no grass in this garden, probably few big bushes and little mud. My gardening shoes may no longer be perfect. I think I'll go buy a pair of white Keds.

Voice and Tone of "Gardening Shoes"

Maryann Macdonald's engaging voice in this piece is one of an experienced storyteller. The tone is friendly. At the beginning, she tells the reader, in the voice of a friend sitting across a small table at lunch, that "the concept of having shoes just for gardening never occurred to me before I lived in England."

The ease with which we hear the flow of this authorial voice makes it look and sound simple to write. The tone of the piece is especially intimate when the writer addresses the reader directly, as she does twice. The first is when she describes her floral Kenzo jeans ("anyone remember those?") and the second, taking a cue from Charlotte Brontë, is when she writes about buying a fountain and finding something else: "Reader, I bought it, and then guess what I found?"

We must, of course, rush to the next paragraph.

But behind this charm is three decades of hard work. That means sitting alone at a desk, writing stories.

Why the Shoes in "Shoes"?

Think of all the objects, plants, tools, and clothes related to your own history with gardens. You could choose one small thing to elevate in order to communicate and illuminate thirty years of a gardening life. What the essayist Phillip Lopate calls the "taste for littleness" in essays is often critical to a piece of personal writing. The little can resonate and speak for the largeness of life.

Maryann could have written an essay called "Gardens I Have Known." She's an experienced and skilled writer — such an essay might have been a good read. Instead, however, she has forever changed our habit of taking for granted what we wear on our feet when mucking about in the garden. She has the ability, as good essayists do, "to turn anything close at hand into a grand meditational adventure" (Lopate again).

Yet the shoes in this piece are not just for meditation. They are a crucial element in the organization and structure of the essay.

Organization and Structure, Rhythm and Compression

There are twelve paragraphs in this essay. Their sequence is determined by chronology. Telling stories chronologically can be risky because the essay may fall into the rut of "then we did this, and then we did that," which often turns out to be an organizational strategy for putting readers to sleep.

But in Maryann's piece, she keeps her focus on what are on her feet during childhood, adolescence, early adulthood, early to middle motherhood, and on into her fifties. But the focus is even tighter and more precise than shoes. She is looking at what are on her feet as she goes about the business of gardening in Detroit, in Washington, D.C., and in London.

This essay is a masterpiece of compression. In eight short paragraphs we have accompanied the writer from childhood through her forties. We learn where she lived, what she was doing, when she had children, when they grew up, and what she planted and cut down. She tells us briefly about how her gardening shoes fit into their moment of history, and into her own nature. She even tells us about those stiletto heels she wore during her brief stint as a non-gardener.

What I have learned from Maryann's other writing is that children's literature, her particular genre, is a form of poetry. Poets are skilled at this kind of compression — a universe expressed in a few words. These are the skills Maryann brings to bear on this essay: compression, rhythm, and detail. Look at the last three sentences at the end of the first paragraph:

> There were shoes for school, playing in, and church/parties —
> that was it. Life was simple. You ate your raspberries off the bush.

You can clap out the rhythm of these three spare sentences. This is Maryann's voice on the page. The sentences are not bogged down with subordinate clauses or elaborate description. The third sentence delivers a simple image that is loaded with associations having a direct relationship to nature and to life.

The sentences are not the only rhythm to admire in this piece. The entire essay flows with the grace of a skater skimming on a frozen pond. One paragraph leads to another, just as one decade in the writer's life leads to the next.

Transitions and Undercutting

Transitional sentences and phrases are critical to "Gardening Shoes." Smooth transitions are important to a reader, who expects to follow one idea to another with ease.

Transitions are especially critical in short essays in which the passage of time is swift and delineated in few words. The last thing a writer wants is to have the reader scratching her head, wondering how in the world the writer got from an

L-shaped garden to a long, narrow Victorian one. Transitions in writing are most noticeable in their absence.

Let's look more closely at this essay. Maryann begins paragraph four with the sentence: "My gardens in England were different." If this sentence were simply floating around without context, we would ask the obvious question: different from what? But we know what she means. She is referring to her patch of melons and azaleas in Washington mentioned in the essay's preceding paragraph. The sentence is used as a transition from one thought—and in this instance, from one country's gardens—to another.

Another device known to skilled writers is *undercutting*. Undercutting wakes up the reader. The writer undercuts (negates) what she has just said. It's a technique that lets readers hear a writer questioning herself. It's also a tool a writer uses to deflate an idyllic situation or to let the air out of a fanciful thought, including fanciful thoughts about the writer herself.

In the penultimate paragraph of "Gardening Shoes," Maryann's gardening life comes together. Everything is perfect: She finds the ideal French gardening shoes, and her Victorian garden, after years of work, is complete with a fountain and flawless summer weather.

A less experienced writer might have been tempted to end an essay there. But the essayist must tell the truth. The writer undercuts the entire essay — for it is, up to this point, a quest for perfection — with the truth, in five words:

> Then we decided to move.

Show, Don't Tell

"Show, don't tell" is a hackneyed phrase in the writing world. Teachers repeat it to nine-year-olds and to writers with advanced degrees. Like most enduring clichés, it is shot full of truth.

A beginning writer might start an essay about a similar subject with: "Gardening has been important to me since I was a child. I like to watch things grow. This has continued throughout my life, and I can say this because I am now in my fifties."

There is nothing wrong with these sentences. But they are bland and conventional. They do not engage the reader's heart, spirit, intellect, or curiosity. They simply tell, in summary form, the writer's connection to gardening. The sentences could apply to any of tens of thousands gardeners in the English-speaking world.

It's the showing that gives the essay the signature, the individuality, of the writer. The writer is in charge of designing the message the reader will receive. The writer will deliver the information so that the reader can add up the details and make up her own mind about what the writer is saying.

With storytelling, it's the showing and feeling about the specific that counts. The writer/narrator has a stake in the story and its outcome. If she cares, really cares, we readers do too. In "Gardening Shoes" the showing starts immediately with the child wearing her blue Keds or her brown school shoes planting that pussy willow or digging out dandelions.

Subtext

The narrative proceeds with specific image after specific image. The writer stays true to her subject, gardening shoes, yet important small revelations about her are layered into the text. Once the writer has children, they are the polestars of her life. Several references to her daughters — as babies, as youngsters, as on-the-cusp adolescents — add depth and color to the essay, revealing what is closest to the writer's heart.

When the reader begins solving the calculus of piece, a portrait of the writer and her concerns emerges. I know what I feel as a reader of this essay about gardening shoes. I feel that the theme — that is, the true subtext of the piece — is loss. It's about acceptance of loss, the transitory nature of life and of things, and hopefulness about the future. These aspects of loss drive the essay and give the writing meaning, depth, and resonance. They are the overarching concerns of gardeners and of practitioners of the art of living.

The writer ends the essay with references to its beginning. She has made a circle of her gardening life. She is ready to start over again, and wonders if it's time for another pair of Keds.

EXAMPLE

This essay was written by Marty Ross, and was published in the "Cuttings" column in the *New York Times* on March 19, 2000. It's a personal essay, also about change, loss, and hope, but it's quite different from Maryann Macdonald's essay in its arc. Marty Ross is writing about a fifteen-month period in her life. She is making her observations from a specific point of view — literally, from a window in her Copenhagen apartment.

A Windowsill Garden with Danish Allure

My husband and I left our big American garden behind at the end of May, when the rosebuds were about to burst, to move to Denmark on a 15-month assignment. Everyone lives in apartments in Copenhagen, and I'm finding the transition from a garden outside to one on table tops and windowsills a little tricky. The scale and the focus are altogether different from what I'm used to in the Midwest, but nevertheless, I'm putting a garden together here.

We found a fine apartment, with tall, bright double windows that capture, in the windows of apartments across the way, the Danish indoor gardening style. If I were an old-fashioned Dane, I'd buy three matching plants, as all my neighbors have done, and place each of them in an identical cachepot in the exact center of each living room window. The arrangement I've ended up with is a little more fluid and organic.

Most of our apartment's windows face northwest, but we're on the fourth floor, just under the attic apartment, and the place is full of soft Scandinavian light. There's no depth to my garden, because the windowsills are only six inches deep, but it is silhouetted against a 19th-century view of stucco buildings with steep red tile roofs and dormer windows, and behind them, a green copper church spire with a weather vane like a golden banner against the clouds roaring in from the North Sea. The garden stretches like a parade from window to window and room to room. When we moved in, magpies were nesting in the top of a locust tree in our little square, and swallows came diving across every day at dusk, practically touching our windowpanes on their way up to nests under the tiles.

One Saturday at the flea market, I snapped up a free-standing planter — a stylish bit of 1950's Danish design in cherry veneer, lined with zinc. The local grocery store happened to be offering flats of boxwood cuttings, and I planted a small hedge in my new trough.

Opposite the boxwood, on the coffee table, I placed a fine prayer plant (Ctenanthe burle-marxii) I bought at a flower stall at the vegetable market. Our apartment is painted white throughout, and the prayer plant's striking stripes had quite an impact. After poking around in the plant shops, which seem to be everywhere here, I found an excellent companion, an Alocasia amazonica, known locally as giraffe plant.

Chalk-white veins divide the Alocasia's leathery, deep green leaves into large rectangles. From the back, the leaves look like big purple hearts, which complement the wine-colored undersides of the prayer plant's foliage. I'm more for balance than symmetry, and the combination looks to me like a stroke of genius.

The Alocasia came with a spider. She was no bigger than a sesame seed, but she spun a delicate web among its slender stems and seemed to feel right at home. It's not very buggy in Copenhagen, even in the summer, so we snag fruit flies for her in the kitchen and toss them into her web. She spins a nice bold stripe in her web from time to time, but we do not know what she means by this.

Healthy indoor plants don't really need much attention, it turns out, but I make the rounds every day, just as I like to do in my garden at home. I poke down into the soil, just to get my fingers dirty, and sometimes tip the plants out of their pots, to admire the roots.

I didn't get to plant seeds at home last spring, but I bought some seeds at the botanic garden here and tacked the packages to my bulletin board. When summer turned to fall, I missed the familiar heft of daffodil bulbs, but my pockets rattled with chestnuts, acorns and bits of lichen on twigs that I picked up under the magnificent trees in the King's Garden, a wonderful park two blocks from our apartment.

Pots of spring-flowering bulbs of every description started popping up at the flower stalls in November. During the holidays, paperwhites reached halfway up our windows. We buy plastic pots stuffed with small bulbs, three pots for $5, and have had the pleasure of sitting at the windows with pale grape hyacinths on long, graceful green stems, dangling snowdrops, little checkered fritillarias and bright yellow winter aconites at our shoulders.

In the dining room, where I have my desk, the windowsills are particularly full at the moment, although I have to leave a window by my desk unobstructed because the Queen's guard marches past at 11:37 every morning in bearskin hats, and I like to lean out and listen to the band, which is exceedingly sharp. There is a fancy little myrtle in the corner window, clipped like a poodle's tail, and a small Christmas poinsettia, still brilliant in the soft gray light. I have a weakness for woody plants, so I bought two dark hollies in tiny pots. I scattered small alder cones from the botanic garden around them on the windowsill, and it looks very woodsy.

I established my shade garden in the guest room, which has the largest windowsills but the least light. Here I grow a strange fern with nearly blue fronds shaped like big, fat T's, possibly Quercifilix zeylanica, and a terra-cotta tray of moss, which the Danes like to use in their Christmas arrangements. I started refreshing it with water as the holidays wore on, and it responded so well that I've kept it.

I've finally taken the plunge for a couple of orchids, which I've always been too much in awe of to try to grow. A white Phalaenopsis, which didn't seem happy in a cool window, has found its place on my desk, where the snow-white flowers have opened one by one above my lamp like fantastic moons. I'm determined to move it back to a windowsill when the weather warms up, but it's almost time to start seeds, and I'm going to need the space. We'll be here until August, and I have it in mind to try some tomatoes.

Voice, Tone, and Scope

The first paragraph, the lead, of this personal narrative sets its tone. The writer gives us the facts: She's in Copenhagen for a fifteen-month assignment, she's left behind a big garden in the Midwest, and her transition to a small indoor garden in a city apartment is "tricky." Nonetheless, she's making the effort.

I particularly admire the subtlety of the submerged humor of the second paragraph. Instead of complaining about the rigidity and repetitiveness of the conventions of the "Danish indoor gardening style," she merely acknowledges it: "If I were an old-fashioned Dane," she writes, she would do the same as her neighboring windowsill gardeners. Then there's a lovely understatement a reader might glide over: "The arrangement I've ended up with is a little more fluid and organic." Marty Ross has delivered her judgment. She has revealed herself. Understatement is a wry, powerful tool in an essay, and a great pleasure for the reader.

The writer's matter-of-fact tone continues throughout the piece. It's a "let-me-tell-you-straight-what-I-am-seeing" voice. Here it is in paragraph 11. The writer has left the window by her desk unobstructed by plants so she can lean out to hear the Queen's guard, a band that passes by "at 11:37 every morning." The band is "exceedingly sharp," she writes — and she's not referring to their snappy bearskin hats, but to their musical ability. There's the undercurrent of subtle judgment again.

Focus: Windowsills and Tabletops

Readers can see that Marty Ross is doing her best to acquire the "taste for littleness" as Lopate puts it, literally and figuratively. The essay is contained, for the most part, as she herself is, within the small space of her apartment and to what she can see out her window. Her "garden" is contained too. She tends to tiny plants in small pots on six-inch windowsills, on a zinc planter, and on her desk. There's no room for rioting plants or riotous Americans in this culture of neat, trim gardening styles and precision marching bands.

The focus in the essay is tight as she details her tiny garden. Whenever the action of the piece goes outside the apartment, to a grocery store, for example, the trip is barely mentioned, yet it serves to feed the subject at hand.

The subject, the indoor garden, also functions to structure the piece. The writer never takes her eyes away from what she observes around her.

The details mark the writer's style. She writes of the "striking stripes" of the prayer plant; "chalk-white veins" dividing the Alocasia's "leathery, deep green leaves"; a spider "no bigger than a sesame seed," which spins a "nice bold stripe in her web"; and "a fancy little myrtle in the corner window, clipped like a poodle's tail."

The writer's sentences and paragraphs sing with images. What is a right image? It's one the reader isn't expecting. It's fresh. It's not a cliché. It's that orchid on her desk whose flowers are opening "one by one . . . like fantastic moons."

An original image is made from the full engagement of the five senses. What do you see? What can you smell, touch, hear, feel? The writer puts herself into the moment.

Scene and Subtext

"A Windowsill Garden with Danish Allure" is a masterful exercise in setting a scene. A reader can "see" in her mind's eye this fourth-floor apartment "just under the attic." It's full of "soft Scandinavian light" from "tall, bright double windows."

The only two pieces of furniture we know about are the writer's desk and her flea market treasure, "a free-standing planter." Yet the rest of the apartment's décor is easily imagined. Why doesn't the writer tell us about everything else in the living room if she's so keen on setting the scene?

A good writer practices restraint. What would be the point in a furniture inventory? Such a list would take the reader away from the central point of this compressed narrative. We get the picture. The writer has told us about two pieces of furniture and that's enough. The two objects serve as a stage for her garden. That's the writer's purpose in showing them to us. Her point here is that she will satisfy her gardening desires, no matter how small and limited her opportunities. That's part of her theme.

Writers learn early on that in "creative" writing, subtext arises from the carefully observed details of real life. The writer writes about what she sees, and in the way she writes about what she sees, readers begin to understand how she feels.

How a writer writes about what she sees is a crucial element in building narrative. The way the writer frames the scene is as important as framing an image through the viewfinder of a camera. The writer, like the photographer, is the decision maker. She directs readers to see what she wants us to see. She builds her theme in this way. Writing is another way of framing the world.

Self-Revelation

Without self-revelation, a personal essay is just a writing exercise. Self-revelation defines the genre. Some writers deliver news from the inner life directly, but many engage in subtle veiled dances with the reader. ("One great use of words is to hide our thoughts," Voltaire wrote.)

When Marty Ross comments dryly that the unfailingly punctual marching band outside her window is "exceedingly sharp," she delivers a judgment on Danish culture in general. But do we learn about the writer herself? This is the heart of the personal narrative and the strength of writing that allows readers to add up details and feelings to get a glimpse of the writer's inner landscape.

Marty Ross is a writer and a gardener paying attention. She feels the deep connection gardeners have with living things. She is away from the spaciousness of her midwestern garden, but she will not go without satisfying her passion. She pokes her fingers into her tiny plant pots in an attempt to get her fingers dirty; she "sometimes tips the plants out of their pots, to admire their roots."

With this small admission, we understand that the writer is full of passionate longing. But we also feel her hopefulness. The *Phalaenopsis* is blooming. She's going to start seeds; she might try some windowsill tomatoes. She is preparing for the new life spring brings. This is her theme. It's the theme of generations of gardeners around the world.

A Note on the Genre

The two essay examples in this chapter are examples of compression and restraint.

But an essayist also writes in wonderfully discursive ways, taking readers on a trip around the writer's world and beyond to arrive back on point. It's not a matter of finding a "correct" way to write an essay. The essay is a work of art requiring patience and practice. That means sitting in a room by yourself, not knowing where you are going, and being strong, to paraphrase a fine writer and teacher, Ron Carlson.

You may be puzzled by the "not knowing where you are going" aspect of the above writing advice. Writers begin essays with strong ideas, don't they? Yes, but the most successful among them write and write until they let go of their preconceived ideas to uncover what is really on their minds.

If this genre appeals to you, read deeply within it. Find a few essays you particularly love. Read them several times, then make a narrative map of one or two, paragraph by paragraph. Note how the writer has delivered the material to the reader. Look at the transitions; hear the tone and voice. You'll be reading as a writer reads.

CHAPTER SEVEN

Pruning and Patience: On Editing and Revision

The true gardener (and writer), to paraphrase Vita Sackville-West yet again, must be brutal and imaginative, to which I would add thick-skinned. If you seek out an opinion about your work, professional or not, the opinion you receive will be based on words and ideas. The opinion is not based on the writer's personality, goodness, garden tidiness, singing voice, spiritual growth, cleanliness, or cooking ability. You want to know how you come across on the page. It's difficult to know this without seeking an opinion — or another set of eyes, as writers often say.

I suspect you have sought the opinion of other gardeners when making decisions about your garden. Perhaps you have hired a professional from time to time. If a garden designer suggests you rip out all those tired daylilies, you likely won't take offense.

But before you bring in others for advice on your writing, there are practical ways for you to begin to edit your own work. Have no fear about pruning your writing, whether it is a how-to article or a personal narrative. Here are some tips to get you started.

Basic Editing

1. *Let your manuscript cool off.* In the pre-computer days, it was suggested you put what you'd written in a desk drawer. It's still a good idea. Print it out and

put it away, at least overnight. Then edit from the printed page. (A different orientation to the words is helpful. I usually take the printed manuscript elsewhere to edit — a different room, a library, a café.)

2. *Read aloud.* You won't believe how helpful this can be. You'll see and hear errors, along with awkward, and perhaps unnecessary, phrases, sentences, and even paragraphs. Even better, read aloud to another person.

3. *Know what to look for.* The craft of writing is complex. As an editor, you should know the rules and regulations (not all of them rigid) to help you polish your work. Be on the lookout for these trouble spots.

- Missing words: Are sentences complete? It's easy to have left out an article adjective or even a verb. It was in your head, but just didn't make it to the fingertips.
- Double words: These are easy easy to fix.
- Repetitive words: Look for the same words (in whatever form) in sentences, paragraphs, and pages. If you see *cut, cutting,* and *cuttings* in a cluster, rewrite to use only one form of the word.
- Unnecessary words: Ferret out those references to "greenhouse facility." It's a greenhouse. Use *Bryson's Dictionary of Troublesome Words* as your bible.
- Punctuation: Most of us don't remember the rules. Do the best you can, then consult a handbook or an editor. (*Bryson's* has a brief punctuation appendix.)
- Verb tense: Articles and essays are usually written in the simple past tense. Make sure the verbs in your manuscript match up. "She thought . . ." "He said . . ."
- Verb agreement: Can be tricky. Search out the obvious disagreements in number between subject and verb. Then, be suspicious. Do you know which collective nouns require singular verbs and under what conditions?

  Example: The herd of sheep keeps the meadow clear. (The collective noun *herd* takes a singular verb in this context.) *BUT:*

  The herd of sheep have scattered. (The collective unit, the herd, has now broken up; a plural verb is required.)

Seek out a handbook or a copy editor. Only the specialized reader knows these grammatical subtleties.

• Spelling: If you use a computer, by all means employ your electronic spellchecking feature. But don't rely on it. If you type *too* but you meant *two,* the spellchecker won't pick up the contextual error.

• Clichés: Books on editing and handbooks for writers have lists of clichés. I find it helpful to look at these lists and note my favorite phrases. They're easier to spot in my writing when my conscience has been pricked by a wiser mind. (Newspaper writing in this country is going to the dogs, don't you think?)

• Repetitive ideas: Look for more than mere repetition of words. What about repetitive ideas? Are you saying the same thing as you have previously but in different words?

Revision Techniques

Judicious picking through a manuscript for obvious errors (editing) is different from rethinking, recasting, reworking, and revising.

Early drafts capture what is at the top of a writer's mind. Subsequent drafts are a gathering in, so to speak, of more-complex elements of the writer's thinking and the writer's knowledge (leavened, depending on the purpose of the writing, by the writer's heart and feelings).

Consider these three techniques after you and your manuscript have cooled from the heat of composition:

• Try out a number of lead paragraphs and ending paragraphs. You may be able to open up your thinking along with the structure of your article or essay.

• Ask yourself if what is on the page is what you meant to say. (The answer to this question for me is often: Not really.)

• Find helpful readers. (Caveat: Not everyone is a helpful reader.)

Revising the Personal Narrative

Reworking the personal narrative requires a deeper kind of revision.

Look at the word itself: RE-VISION. You are looking again. You are seeing again, looking back and reexamining. Art is born in the revision.

In early drafts, writers are clearing their throats for what will come. When you rethink, you will find the spine of what you are after and then you will know where to go.

Maxine Hong Kingston, who wrote the breathtaking memoir *The Woman Warrior,* gives this advice to writers in her latest book, *The Fifth Book of Peace:*

> Each time you rewrite, you're going back into the tunnels, bringing more knowledge out . . . You shine more light on some question, problem, hard time, suffering, memory, ignorance . . .
> The story changes as you change. And history changes too . . .

Going deeper: This is the reason for the personal narrative.

You are not "correcting" anything in your re-visioning. You are listening to your piece to see if it wants something more. What are you holding back?

Imagination must sit on your shoulder to help memory. Writers often say: "But that's how I remember what happened." They are remembering a string of events. But readers want more. They want to understand not just what happened but also what it meant — to the characters involved, a family, a community, a country. Writing personal narrative has been called "inventing the truth." You are after the truth of your experience; you must take us, your readers, with you. We want to know everything you saw, tasted, heard, touched, smelled. Who spoke? Who walked across the street? Who tripped? Who left and didn't return?

Inventing the Truth

Maxine Hong Kingston is one of the late-twentieth-century's greatest writers. She was born in 1940 in California, but is steeped in her Chinese ancestral history through family stories. (If you haven't read *The Woman Warrior,* I suggest you do so.) She wasn't present when most of the events of the book took place. She didn't see the people of her father's village attack the family home or witness the destruction of her grandparents' rice crop. She wasn't even born.

So how could she write about what happened with this level of detail?

I can't answer this question for Maxine Hong Kingston. But I can suggest ways other writers have approached "inventing the truth."

- Listen to family stories. Ask questions about geography, climate, time, food, crops, building materials, clothing — all the elements that make up human life. Ask everyone, even unreliable narrators. Take notes. (Memories will vary, of course, but this won't matter.)
- Research contemporary accounts of the era that interests you. Do this even if you were there, and even if family members are still around to interview. Consult a research librarian. Read multiple sources, including newspapers. If you can't remember what plants were in your great-grandmother's garden, you can read the garden journals of the day, taking into consideration the climate in which she lived and the availability of fresh foods for purchase. Historians write about these things too. Search them out.

When to Call in an Expert: Copy Editing

An experienced copy editor will read your text and correct it for grammatical, spelling, syntactical (the way words are put together), and other errors, such as spacing. She may also make queries or comments in the text.

I don't want to seem unkind or snooty about your sister-in-law who is "good at writing" and who has offered to make corrections for you. Thank her, but forget it. You need an expert.

But when do you need a copy editor? Do you need one if you have been asked to send a short article to a local paper or to a local newsletter?

The answer is not definitive. A local newspaper will have a copy editor but a free "shopper" weekly may not. No matter where your article appears, you want it to be as error-free and clear as possible.

If what you have written is intended for a small and personal readership within a circle of family members and friends, it's still a good idea to have what you have written professionally edited.

Inevitably, when I enter in the corrections made by my beloved copy editor, I rethink certain ideas and passages. The text may deepen, become clearer, or both.

Many copy editors, but not all, will edit on disk, entering in the corrections for you. This is how the world is going, but this is not how I work. I'm in there digging through the text myself. But with computer-based editing, all changes are either in color or underlined, so they show. You might love it.

When to Call in an Expert: Content Editing

When an author writes an in-depth article or a book within a specialized field, the manuscript is read for "content" by experts. A book on the propagation of herbs, for example, would be read by a botanical editor, and/or by other experts on the propagation of herbs.

These readers are looking at ideas and information. They raise questions about matters of fact.

Nonprofessional Readers: Boon or Bane?

Many professional writers never show a work in progress to family members. Husbands and wives and partners read the work when everyone else does, when the writing is in print.

Some writers, on the other hand, see their spouse as critical to the development of their work.

So how are you, who may be a beginning writer, to make your way through this minefield of curious eyes?

Through experience, I know that in composing a text, writers are also composing a self. Family members are not objective readers. This composition of a self is a delicate matter.

Instead find, or start, a writing group. Your writing persona should be protected within a circle of like-minded people. These fellow or sister writers will understand that what they are reading is part of a long apprenticeship and that you are on a step-by-step journey into your writing self. They'll understand because they are on the same path.

So: Protect yourself. Seek readers with empathy, expertise, and objectivity.

CHAPTER EIGHT

Leafing Out in Public: Is Publishing for You?

Newsletter and newspaper editors have space to fill and deadlines to meet. Always on the lookout for how-to articles, features, book reviews, and brief news pieces, editors may be looking for you.

How Will Editors Find You?

Some gardeners seem to fall into publishing opportunities. A designer and grower was tapped to write an introduction to an anthology. He rose to the occasion. Another garden designer was offered a weekly gardening column. Master Gardeners may fulfill community service obligations by writing columns and articles.

But if you are a gardener who wants to write about what you know and love, waiting to be discovered is not a reliable strategy. You must seek out the publication and then write, in the form of a query letter, to the editor. From the *Fiddlehead Forum* (the bulletin of the American Fern Society) to *Plants and People* (the biannual newsletter of the Society for Economic Botany), there is a publication for you.

Finding Publications

To find publications, use:
- Your computer
- Your library
- Your library's databases

Your own computer is a good starting point. Use a search engine like Google to discover what it can offer you.

For example, you know that plant societies have at least one publication, if not more. They may be organized on local, state, and national levels. If you enter "plant society" into Google, you will come up with the first ten of 170,000 sites. When the field is narrowed to "plant societies + salvia," 3,430 entries pop up. (Who can resist reading about "psychoactive" gardening and *Salvia divinorum*?)

The *reference section of your local library* will help you stay on task. A college or university library may be of even more assistance with deeper and more up-to-date resources.

In an earlier era, a leisurely visit to a library's current periodical section would have borne fruitful ideas. Such a visit may still prove profitable, but it won't give you the whole picture. Many publications are now published online only.

When you look for garden-related publications, you will find they fall into a number of categories:

1. Consumer publications (newspapers and popular magazines like *Better Homes and Gardens*)
2. Trade publications (*Nursery Management and Production* is an example)
3. Association publications *(Fiddlehead Forum)*
4. Scientific publications *(Plant Physiology)*

Databases and *specialty reference books* categorize and list publications. They can help you find the names of garden- and plant-related print and electronic periodicals. Some libraries may have the print version of the following reference materials (make sure to check the date), and others will have these available as electronic databases. Here are the most commonly used:

- *Magazines for Libraries*
- *Ulrich's International Periodical Directory*
- *Bacon's Media Directory*

These reference materials list publications by category. Study the categories before you start. Categories will exist for Garden, Home, Agriculture, and Botany, among other fields. Start with *Magazines for Libraries*. It is the most accessible of the guides; the other two mentioned above list thousands of periodicals and can be overwhelming at first.

Most libraries will have *The Guide to Information Sources in the Botanical Sciences,* by Elisabeth Davis and Diane Schmidt. Although somewhat out of date, it is an important book listing indexes, journals, bibliographies, and databases about plants and related subjects. It will give you an overview of how botanical information is organized.

Another helpful reference book is the *Encyclopedia of Associations.* In it, you can find listings of specific plant societies. Once you have the names of those that interest you, you can look them up online to check for the existence of a newsletter or other periodical.

Knowing the Publication and Writer's Guidelines

Editors are busy people. They don't have time to read or to respond to queries from writers or would-be writers who haven't done their homework. If you suggest a story on medicinal herbs to a newsletter that covers woody plants, you are wasting your time and the editor's. If you suggest a two-thousand-word story to a publication that publishes brief (five-hundred-word) articles, or you propose an article on a subject that was recently covered, you are likewise revealing that you have not studied the publication.

Printed publications often have a Web site for promotional reasons. You can search a site for an idea of the purpose and format of a publication. An electronic publication, even if its content is available only to subscribers, will have sample stories to read free of charge.

Most publications have writer's or editorial guidelines. Often, writer's guidelines are bullet-pointed suggestions from the editors to would-be contributors explaining what the publication is looking for in an article. Some are available online, or send an e-mail addressed to the editor.

Some writer's guidelines are vague; others are quite helpful. The following guidelines are directed to contributors to the trade magazines published by

Branch-Smith Inc. The firm publishes *Nursery Management and Production,* *Greenhouse Management and Production,* and other journals.

I admire these guidelines. They are upbeat but at the same time sharp and precise.

The guidelines appear here courtesy of Branch-Smith and Todd Davis, editor of *Nursery Management and Production:*

Editorial Guidelines

To achieve the Branch-Smith Inc. Editorial Mission Statement of being "must-read" publications for the horticulture industry, these editorial guidelines have been developed for the company's magazines. These guidelines will allow the magazines to deliver information in a "ready-to-use" format and to speak authoritatively.

14 ways to write a better service journalism story!

1. Know what the editor wants. Make sure you understand specifically what the editor wants the story to be about when it is assigned. Find out whether the editor has specific sources in mind for you to contact. This can save you a lot of time and frustration.

2. Put readers first. Find subjects they want to know about and present those subjects simply, quickly and attractively. Save the reader time by being clear and concise. Personalize the story and involve the reader, use second person when appropriate. Personalize the story even further by writing in the first person: "How we achieve disease-free cuttings at Oglevee Ltd." Emphasize how-to and concrete benefits. You want the story to move the reader to some action.

3. Don't preach. The reader is your colleague and contemporary. Although you are sharing information with readers that they need to know, in many cases you just learned it yourself from your source.

4. Know your audience. What is it about your story that readers really need to know? How can the story benefit them? Envision the person you are writing to. Is it a retailer, greenhouse grower or nursery grower? Write like you are talking to the reader.

5. Organize your thoughts. Have some idea of where you want the story to go before you call your first source. Think in terms of how and why the person you're interviewing did something.

6. Formulate questions with service journalism in mind. Remember you want the source to provide answers that can be presented simply, quickly and attractively. Examples: What are the three things you do to ensure you have an adequate number of poinsettia cuttings? What are the five best annuals that you produce for hot, dry locations? By asking these types of questions it will require less time for you to organize your notes into a service journalism article.

7. Headlines, blurbs and leads. Get to the point quickly. Write short, punchy, and aggressively. Make them benefit-oriented. Some phrases to consider include: Ways to . . .; Pointers on . . .; Quick . . .; Easy . . .; Handy . . .; Low-cost ways to . . .; Profit-building . . .; Money-saving . . . or Money-making . . .; A better way to . . . When possible, write "how to" headlines without using "how to." Blurbs should help tease readers into the story.

8. Simplify the presentation. Write shorter stories and more of them. Divide the information into manageable bites. The recommended length of a main or feature story should be 12 to 20 inches, depending on the editor's discretion.

9. Devices, techniques and other gimmicks. Consider using these to make your story more service-oriented and aid in reader comprehension. Not every story has to contain all of these elements, but the more you use, the more usable your information becomes.

Lists: Whenever information lends itself to a list make one (dos, don'ts, 6 ways to . . .). Checklists are handy. Number the steps, use bullets, pointing fingers or check marks as appropriate.

Subheads: When appropriate try to insert a subhead every 3 to 5 inches. They provide entry points for skimmer readers, provide graphic relief to the reader's eye and call attention to important information in the article. Make subheads benefit-oriented.

Fact and bio boxes: Company history and specifics (size of operation, number of locations, crops produced, etc.) can be deleted from the main story and included in a fact box.

Q&A: This can be used throughout the article or with a sidebar to cover one specific topic.

References: Lists of suppliers of products mentioned in story with reader inquiry number or addresses when appropriate.

Other: Quizzes ("Check your knowledge on . . ."), glossaries, bibliographies, definition boxes, time lines, etc.

10. Sidebars. A long story that is broken into shorter pieces is going to attract more readers. Sidebars should run 3 to 12 inches. If you're not sure whether a story will make an appropriate sidebar, mark it "possible sidebar," and the editor will decide.

11. Graphics, photographs. Think process when taking photographs or considering graphics. If someone is demonstrating a production technique, take a series of photographs that illustrates the procedure pictorially. Photos can be used to illustrate step-by-step and how-to techniques. For retail stories, process is appropriate, but also consider displays, products and overall store image.

12. Cutlines [captions]. Make cutlines informative. Be clear and concise. When possible don't use the same information from the story in the photo cutline. Don't restate what's being shown in the picture unless it is necessary to more clearly describe what is being shown.

13. Informed sources, updates and buzzwords. Save information that won't fit in your story for informed sources and updates. In most cases, you'll have more information from your interviews than space for your stories. It's probably good information that our readers would be interested in. This will also save you time later when you are looking for informed sources and update topics.

14. Stories don't have to be dry and boring! Let your stories reflect your personality, writing style, and expertise. Don't be afraid to let the reader know you are knowledgeable.

Finding Your Subject

It's worth repeating: Focus your articles.

Beginning writers may find this difficult. Students' topics are often too abstract, vague, or broad.

Let's say you want to write an article about how many gardeners, unconsciously or not, plant what their grandmothers (or grandfathers) did. But unless you plan to write a personal essay, refine and expand your idea to fit the format of a feature article. Interview three gardeners who are conscious of making this link to childhood; interviews will allow you to develop the theme. Focus your article on the stories of the three gardeners. It is your job to weave them together in order to make your point.

If you have a big idea, bring it down to earth with the specific.

The Query Letter: Sending Your Idea to the Editor

Learn the craft of the query letter. You should:

- Address the editor by first and last names
- Submit a single-spaced page (12-point type)
- Impart a professional tone and appearance
- Develop a story idea reflecting a particular angle

- Write clearly and concisely
- Base your idea on the reality of the publication
- Make sure the letter is impeccably edited
- Enclose a self-addressed, stamped envelope (SASE)
- Include clips of relevant, previously published work if possible
- Send it by post or, if acceptable, e-mail it

No matter how small the publication, if you do not already have a relationship with the editor (and even if you do), you should query in this formal, professional manner.

Even though the letter serves to "sell" your idea, do not use phrases like "your readers will love this" and "this is an idea you can't pass up." You are selling your idea with your intelligence and clear thinking, not with advertising slogans and inappropriate assumptions.

Most professional writers work diligently on query letters. They will have researched and fleshed out their subjects. They have read issues of the publication to understand its tone and subject matter.

Writers know they have one minute to entice the editor. The first paragraph of a query letter serves as a hook for a delicious or thought-provoking idea; it is also a sample of the writer's skill.

Once you have a relationship with an editor, you may be able to pitch your idea by telephone, in a one-paragraph e-mail, or by smoke signals. Otherwise, toe the professional line.

Sample Query Letter

This is the query letter that landed the article I wrote in the *New York Times* on Zion National Park.

6 July 2000

Ms. [editor's full name]
The New York Times, Travel Section
229 West 43rd Street
New York, NY 10036

Dear [editor's full name],

No more cars in National Parks! the writer and passionate desert-lover Edward ("Cactus Ed") Abbey thundered more than 30 years ago. *Walk,* cried Abbey, or ride mules, bicycles, or wild pigs — anything but motors.

During my seven-day, early summer hiking trip in Zion National Park, as I rode the fleet of bright new propane-fueled shuttle buses up and down the canyon, I wondered if the prickly spirit of Cactus Ed was the least bit soothed by the new ban on cars in this dusty red and alkali-white canyon. The mandatory shuttle system is the first in the 80-year history of the National Park System. It's an attempt to solve the perennial tension between public access and preservation.

It works. I took the 8.6-mile shuttle loop early in the morning and far into the evening. I took it to one trailhead after another, grateful that I wasn't there the previous year, when I might have been in one of 5,000 cars vying for 450 parking spaces inside the upper portion of the canyon, the primary destination of most of Zion National Park's 2.5 million annual visitors.

My proposed story, about 1,800 words, will focus on the dramatic changes the shuttle system has brought to Zion, in addition to other new services — a sustainable-energy visitors center; a shuttle into Zion's gateway town, Springdale; and the amenities available in Springdale to travelers. Happily, it is no longer necessary to drive 20 minutes to Hurricane or 45 to St. George for peanut butter. I will also explain what exactly one does with the family car at Zion. (I did a careful study of the published guidebooks on Zion National Park — all are out of date.)

I will describe, as a middle-aged solo traveler, my hiking experiences. I took almost every trail in this central part of the canyon, and I did what would have been impossible just one summer earlier — walked up-canyon along the road, following the river, a sojourn interrupted only by the occasional shuttle bus, with its driver waving a friendly hello.

I am coauthor of two books on the Southwest, both published by Bantam, and I have written one piece on the Southwest for the Travel Section. Most recently, I am publisher and editor of DiRT: *A Garden Journal from the Connecticut River Valley,* two copies of which are enclosed.

Sincerely,

Paula Panich

Why Did This Query Letter Work?

Zion National Park has been written about thousands of times for three quarters of a century; what could be new? Plenty, as it turned out.

The shuttle system had been in operation for less than a week when I arrived. It was the first of the National Park Service's shuttle experiments. This was news travelers could use.

You'll notice that there is a lead paragraph to hook the reader-editor, followed by the all-essential nut graf, the paragraph that contains the kernel of the article's topic.

The two paragraphs contain four sentences. If a writer doesn't deliver in four sentences, the idea may be lost on the editor or on the editorial assistant, who may be weeding out obvious rejects from the query pile.

This letter may seem simple to you. It wasn't simple to write. I had read books about Zion and about Utah, including two on geology and botany; I had spent seven days hiking and observing; I had studied the Park Service's information. I had talked to park interpreters and rangers — how was I to write a six-paragraph query letter?

I knew from years of reading the Travel Section, and from having published an article in the section previously, that the editors want useful articles. Readers of the Travel Section of the *Times* expect to be able to follow in the footsteps of the writer. The idea for the article had to be boiled down to its essence and then presented in a lively way.

There is a craft to the query letter. Writers don't all construct these letters in the same way, of course, but let's look at those six paragraphs from the point of view of sequence and content:

1. Lead paragraph (the hook)
2. Nut graf (the essentials)
3. Amplification of the nut graf
4. Proposal paragraph (length of piece included)
5. Additional aspect of story clarified
6. Qualifications paragraph

Do you have to deliver exactly what your query letter suggests? Yes and no. My story on Zion (see chapter 5) does address the new shuttle system as an important element of the story. The shuttle system is the news hook. The editors would not have been happy if the news had been buried in the piece or otherwise given short shrift.

Although I worked very hard on the first two paragraphs of the query, I didn't use them as the lead in the article. You don't have to be married to your query letter, just loyal to it in spirit.

Writing a Column: A Commitment Akin to Marriage

If an editor engages you to write a column, take that word *engages* seriously. Columnists have to be committed to a never-ending deadline. Writing a weekly column is more pressure than a monthly column, of course, but either way, examine your motivation behind accepting the responsibility.

Income is not likely to be it. Most columnists in smaller publications receive a pittance and some work for free (though that's not a recommended course of action).

So what will be your motivation for writing a column? Columns are opinion pieces. It's satisfying to share your thoughts and insights with readers. You are making a community for yourself. If you are a garden designer and your income is related to the subject at hand, writing a column can be an important element in your overall effort to make your work known.

Columnists have great fun. But you might run out of ideas fast at the beginning.

Then what? Then you have to start thinking like a writer. This is the part of the commitment that won't go away. You will learn to scan the universe looking for events, people, trends, and ideas that will be grist for your column mill. Then you will separate the chaff from the wheat and — write the piece to make deadline.

And you must always make deadline. No exceptions.

What Happens When Your Work Is Edited?

A professional garden designer who has just begun to write about plants and gardens recently called. She was perplexed. Her two articles, once they were published, were almost unrecognizable as her work. What was happening? she asked.

My guess is that despite her degree in English, she wasn't writing in journalistic style or in the style of the publication.

When I've been edited well, the work improves and I learn more about writing.

When I've been edited by an inexperienced editor, the work (in my humble opinion) suffers.

Either way, the editor is your boss. In smaller publications, you won't see how your piece will be edited until it is in print. If you are consistently edited in ways you find disagreeable, you can speak to the editor about it or choose not to publish there again. Larger publications will almost always show you the final edit before your article goes into print.

Sometimes your article may not be edited except for length. It is up to you to know exactly the word length that is required. Don't exceed it. At times, an editor may decide to trim your article even though you have been meticulous about its required length. It's out of your hands!

What About the Writing Business?

This book is intended to help you get your ideas onto paper. Knowing about the business of writing is critical but not in the scope of this book. I urge you to start on your path to this knowledge by joining the Garden Writers Association. On the Web, visit www.gardenwriters.org. You will learn the difference between selling all rights and first serial rights to your work, as well as what "work-for-hire" means and a guide to current copyright laws.

Publishing Your Own Newsletter or Magazine: A Case History

Pamela Weil began publishing the quarterly newsletter *Connecticut Gardener* in 1995, marrying her two passions: desktop publishing and gardening. The idea for her niche publishing venture came when she read a national magazine cover to cover and found nothing of practical use for "us here in Connecticut," she says.

Pam had learned desktop publishing in 1992. She used her skill for two years at a small local magazine before she stepped out on her own.

"I wore a lot of hats at this publication," Pam says. She set up ads, designed

print promotional material, talked with advertisers, and wrote copy. She loved it all. "The work is very detail-oriented," she says, "but to me it was exhilarating — I loved doing all the pieces that made the publication work."

Then Pam and her husband sat down at the kitchen table to discuss how much money they could afford to lose if Pam started a gardening publication. They agreed on a sum that was "equal to a modest car," she says. "It takes a long time to make any money; you need to count on eight years."

Not that she lost much. Almost immediately, *Connecticut Gardener* paid for itself. But that is because the publisher works from her home. She designs and sets up each of the four annual issues, she solicits and designs the ads. She buys mailing lists of potential subscribers and does the billing. She creates her own advertising materials but pays a printer, a mailing house, and freelance writers.

Nonetheless, "it took eight years for me to get comfortable with the cash flow," she says.

Her knowledge of the desktop publishing tools PageMaker and PhotoShop is critical to her ability to publish *Connecticut Gardener.*

As she begins her ninth year of publication, Pam still loves it. "The most fun I have is changing *Connecticut Gardener* based on subscriber feedback," she says. Recently she has added columns that will run in every issue.

She publishes from March to October. "It allows me to have a life," she says. "Besides, garden centers don't want to advertise all year."

Connecticut Gardener has a Web site Pam uses for promotion of the printed newsletter. What if you were to start a strictly online garden-related magazine? The publishing challenges are similar.

A critical element in your thinking should be the definition of subject matter. Thousands of publications compete for readers online and in print. How will you narrow and focus your subject? The title, *Connecticut Gardener,* leaves little doubt as to the identification of the potential reader, although Pam has many subscribers outside the state who also garden in USDA Zones 5 and 6.

Publishing a periodical on paper or electronically is a high-maintenance endeavor requiring exquisite planning, patience, and vision. But if you love the idea, then you love it, and with dedication, effort, and luck you will persevere.

CHAPTER NINE

You Already Know How Your Garden Grows: Practice, Discipline, and Time

Writing, like gardening, takes practice. But unlike gardening, writing doesn't lend itself to interruptions. It's an impulse that withers quickly when conjoined with the telephone, radio, television; it disappears with the deadlines of breakfast, appointments, dinner, carpools, hungry poodles. Also unlike gardening, composing a text requires sitting still indoors.

You can take notes out in the garden, you can write in a journal out in the garden, but for the actual composition of a draft of a piece of writing, you need:

- ❧ Quiet
- ❧ Solitude
- ❧ Time

All rules have exceptions. Journalists compose in busy newsrooms; Jane Austen, that kitchen-table writer, wrote in the heat of family life; Melville wrote in the belly of a whale.

But my guess is that you haven't tethered yourself to a desk for a long while and are wondering how you'll do it. Although no two writers are alike, and each has famous quirks and tricks to start her writing day, some advice: *Write in the morning.*

Write in the morning before you dress, eat, talk, think. Your mind is fresh. You will be productive. Write in the morning for fifteen minutes, then expand it to thirty.

If you have awakened to a radio blast for twenty years, change your habit. Make the thing buzz instead. You don't want to hear the news; the news will steal your writing mind. So will your spouse, your children, your mother, your neighbor, even your dog and certainly your parrot.

Don't answer the phone. Don't even think of checking the weather by turning on the television.

Where Are You Going to Write?

Writers have hidden away in basements, attics, musty back bedrooms, and mouse-ridden shacks on the ocean cliffs. M. F. K. Fisher often wrote in a rented motel room during the day, returning to her family in the evening. (By the way, writers have written entire books in their pajamas and articles in their underwear.)

Maybe you don't have a shack overlooking the Atlantic. I don't either. That doesn't mean we can't claim a space of our own.

Making a space to write is also claiming psychological space. This will take some finesse if you must write on the computer in a cluttered family room or den.

Roy Peter Clark, journalist and writing teacher, urges writers to "set the table." This is what he means: Before you go to bed, clear the space around the computer. Set out your notes, your books, your writing talismans. (My current talisman: a wooden mask from I don't-know-where, a gift from my daughter.) Prepare yourself. Plant a seed in your mind for what will come in the morning. This is a deeper meaning of to "set the table."

If you are lucky enough to have a desk or a room of your own, this setting of the table is still important. Clear the clutter. Stack the bills elsewhere, file the insurance papers, and sharpen your pencil.

You are removing the printed word from your sight. I often don't allow myself to make a cup of tea in the kitchen until I have written at least twenty or thirty minutes in the spare bedroom–turned–writing room, where I am working on this book. Why would I do this?

Because the kitchen is chockablock with interesting things to read: notes near the phone; recipes taped to the cupboard; spines of cookbooks; new magazines (even a peek can be fatal to the morning's work); and that scourge of all writers, the morning paper. Leave it on the porch until you've written your quota.

Electronic mail is another great consumer of the writing impulse. If you check your e-mail when you sit down at your computer in those precious early moments of consciousness, you're cooked. Some writers check their e-mail once a week. Some writers no longer have e-mail, understanding how easy it is to think they are writing when they are writing e-mail. Reading and writing electronic mail means you are entering the world outside yourself. It's a monstrous maw into which your time and energy can disappear.

Almost all writers are masters of procrastination. I doubt if you will be able to come up with an original writing-avoidance tactic; writing takes steely resolve.

Some writers write at night, like the marvelous novelist Richard Peck. Some writers write only in certain months. Some, like Isabelle Allende, start a new project on the same day each year. And some beginning writers might research how other writers write, spending six months or a year reading up on this crucial subject. They think they're writing, but they're not. Ditto for your devotion to your book group. Reading is critical to a writer's preparation, but it is not the thing itself.

How Long to Write?

Knowing when to stop the day's writing is an art in itself. My editor, John Bowman, reminds me of Hemingway's purported practice and advice: He is said to have started by isolating himself early in the morning and then keeping at writing as long as he felt the ideas and words were flowing. When he got to a point where he felt he still had some good things to say, he would quit for the day. That way he looked forward to starting in on the next.

When you have a few years' experience under your belt, your writing habits change. Complicity, and trust, can be forged between your hand and your mind.

Writers almost always have other jobs. Garden writers are often garden designers, nursery owners, horticulturists, and teachers. Mark Adams, for example, owns acres of greenhouses. He's been writing his gardening column for three decades; he's so adept at it that he often writes from the seat of his tractor. He thinks in the shape of his column after all these years.

The world doesn't want you to be a writer. That's why the craft demands resolve, dedication, steadiness, and discipline.

Journal Keeping

• **Garden journals.** Many gardeners keep a journal of the evolution of their garden. You may be one of them. A garden journal is a record of gardening seasons. Gardeners may keep daily or weekly notes as to weather, what bloomed when, what material was added or subtracted, how the soil was emended, what pests were at work, and when it was time to harvest.

Some gardeners keep an annual paperbound journal; a gardener I know keeps all her notes on a computer, cross-indexed by an alphabetical list of plants. Another gardener keeps an annual journal of photographs of her plants, along with commentary.

A garden journal is crucial to a gardener's desire to build on experience. Gardens are complex. Details of a gardener's work in her garden are difficult to keep in mind from year to year.

One of my garden-writing students found that as she annotated her gardening year, she began to jot down her thoughts and feelings in the journal. The experience inspired her to begin a more personal journal.

• **Other journals.** Even if you keep a gardening journal, you might profit as a writer by keeping some other type of journal as well.

Dozens of books have been published in the past decade or so on the subject of keeping journals.

Journals are kept for a number of reasons. Here's a short list:

➥ Personal journal
➥ Nature journal
➥ Cooking journal
➥ Dream journal
➥ Writer's journal

CULTIVATING WORDS

Decide whether you want to keep a journal. It's a way of delineating the self. If it's true, as a Chinese philosopher once said, that the purpose of life is to see, a journal is a good place to practice the art of close observation. It's also a place to practice the art and craft of writing.

A journal is the writer's equivalent of a visual artist's sketchbook, and, indeed, many journal keepers sketch and write on their blank pages. Doing so doubles your chance of developing a refined awareness of what you see in this physical world.

The purposes of the journals I have listed overlap and join. It's natural to write dreams in the notebook that serves as a personal journal or to take notes from what you have seen in the woods. You can organize your inner and outer lives through these notebooks.

A writer's notebook or journal is a different matter, however. Many writers, while working on a book or other piece of writing, will use a notebook to jot down ideas for the work in progress. A writer deep into a work narrows her vision. The world is scanned for what may attach itself to the work. This is not necessarily intentional, as the mind seems to fold itself around the task. A fiction writer, for example, on a walk in the woods may see in a passing hiker just the right gait for a character in a story.

A writer's notebook can also serve as a general catch basin for writing ideas. He may clip bits of newspaper stories and tape them into his notebook or he may write single lines of ideas: "Article about learning to see."

As one of my writing teachers, the short story master Ron Carlson, says: "Paper is cheap. Your ideas aren't."

Journal keeping is a journey into the world and into your mind. It's an incubator, not a shaped piece of writing in itself. Journal entries are not pieces of writing the world is longing to see (although certain passages may make their way unedited into a piece of finished work) unless you have already won the Nobel Prize in Literature.

• **The Wild Mind journal.** Natalie Goldberg, writer, writing teacher, and painter, has published many books on writing and life. I've read and admired them. My favorite is *Wild Mind: Living the Writer's Life*.

I can recommend this book to you unequivocally. I have used its ideas and methods in my own life and work. I have used it to urge students to write. I've used this book's ideas with fourth-grade students at the American School in London, and with adult students at Canyon Ranch in the Berkshires, with whom I had exactly one hour and fifteen minutes to jump-start their writing.

In fact, just writing about this book this morning has filled my mind with excitement and possibility and makes my hands itch with the desire to write something unexpected and wild — something I don't already know about or have planned.

She suggests taking a word — let's say the noun *compost* (not an abstract noun like *power* or *justice*) and write about this word for a few minutes one morning.

But wait: This won't be an essay on the virtues of composting or a how-to on what to put in the compost pile. It's something else entirely, and it may not be about composting at all. It's about letting go of your precooked ideas and finding out what's hidden in the heart.

Natalie Goldberg offers seven rules for her Wild Mind writings. Here is the first one, in part:

> 1. *Keep your hand moving.* Once you sit down to write, whether it's for ten minutes or an hour, once you begin, don't stop. If an atom bomb drops at your feet eight minutes after you've begun and you were going to write for ten minutes, don't budge . . .

Buy a fresh spiral-bound notebook. Use it for a month for no purpose other than your Wild Mind writing for a month. You will change. Your writing will become deeper and more fluid between day one and day thirty.

But what does Wild Mind writing have to do with writing a gardening column, or anything else? you may well ask yourself. Writing is a journey. No matter your writing task, your prose, not to mention your heart and mind, will be enlivened by a connection to the unexpected in feeling and language.

Here is the poet Gary Snyder, from his essay "Language Goes Both Ways":

> Ordinary Good Writing is like a garden that is producing exactly what you want, by virtue of lots of weeding and cultivating. What you get is what you plant, like a row of beans. But really good

writing is both inside and outside the garden fence. It can be a few beans, but also some wild poppies, vetches, mariposa lilies, ceanothus, and some juncos and yellow jackets thrown in. It is more diverse, more interesting, less predictable, and engages with a much broader, deeper kind of intelligence. Its connection to the wildness of language and imagination helps give it power.

Natalie Goldberg is suggesting is a thirty-day trial engagement with your own wild mind. It can't hurt. Then you can decide if you want to make it a more permanent relationship.

Writing Partners and Writing Groups

If writing is such a solitary business, how does it work to have a writing partner?

If you find the right person, someone of good intention who is as committed as you are to growing as a writer, a writing partnership can be an illuminating and fruitful experience, one that keeps you from feeling too isolated. Make sure your intended partner is a good, if not great, listener with an imagination akin to yours. But how do you structure your writing partnership?

Here are a few ideas. The possibilities of alignment are, of course, unlimited between people of like mind.

- **Café writing.** In the Wild Mind model, you and your partner meet in a café or coffee shop and write together, then read. Good energy can be generated this way. You take turns suggesting a word and the number of minutes you will write on that word.
- **Café meetings.** You and your partner read aloud what each of you has written during the week. Meeting in this way makes the writing real.
- **Letter exchange.** For fifteen years, I have been writing letters to a fellow writer, Mark Greenside, not expecting critique or even comment in return. These letters have never been sent by electronic means. They are mostly handwritten, and written to see what I have on my mind. They often serve to spark my writing.

There's psychological safety in this on a number of levels, but first and foremost is the safety of not swamping myself with plans and fears. Example: When I was hiking in Zion National Park, I didn't want to be thinking about what I might write about it. That would have taken me away from the direct engagement with rocks and water and plants. I wanted to be in the moment, not in the what-am-I-going-to-do-with-all-this-stuff anxiety mode. (I saved that for later.) Instead, I wrote a few lines to Mark in the evenings. That way I preserved some details but didn't allow myself to jump out of the experience into my reporter's brain.

- **Manuscript exchange.** If you and your writing partner have the right chemistry and mutual respect, serving as readers for each other can be useful and even enlightening. I suggest sending off your piece when you feel you have a solid, readable draft, meaning something that feels more or less complete and has been edited for big obvious Mistakes.

Define the intent of your piece to your reader. Tell her what you would like from her reading. Do you want to know if there are missing transitions? Do you want to know if you sound sincere? corny? illogical? Perhaps you just want a spellchecker. Do your reader a favor and ask for what you want. That way you won't be disappointed. It's an honor and a responsibility to be a reader. Don't agree to do it yourself unless you are willing to put in the time and effort it takes to do a proper job.

Writing groups are another matter. A group can be critical to your growth as a writer and is a good way to maintain your commitment to yourself. A writing group that meets once a week or once a month means you have a corresponding deadline.

If you are a beginning writer, I urge you to find a group that is led by a professional writer and an experienced teacher. Workshop critique can be tricky, and you need someone who knows the ropes and will set up guidelines for giving and receiving constructive criticism.

Writing groups are often organized around a specific genre, like fiction writing, or memoirs, or essays. Some are also organized around topics, or a book such as *Wild Mind* or Julia Cameron's *The Artist's Way*.

Start a garden writers group in your area. You will profit from the experience.

However you enter the world of garden writing, remember the garden is not just a metaphor for life — it is life. If not, there wouldn't be millions of us on earth engaging in this physical, spiritual, and intellectual pursuit of cultivating our gardens and, for some of us, our words to describe them.

The secret we gardeners know is this: All the world is a garden. In the garden is found all culture, civilization, human achievement and folly, love and disappointment, the whole lot of what it means to be human and to engage ourselves with nature, which is not separate, after all, from who we are.

Appendix 1

Selected Resources for the Writing Gardener

Four Plant Databases

International Plant Names Index
www.ipni.org

Missouri Botanical Garden Plant Science
www.mobot.org/plantscience

Ohio State University Web Garden
www.webgarden.osu.edu

USDA Plant Database
http://plants.usda.gov

Two Botanical Reference Books

Plant: The Ultimate Visual Reference to Plants & Flowers of the World, by Janet
Marinelli (London: Dorling Kindersley in association with the Royal Botanic
Gardens, Kew, 2004)

The American Horticultural Society A–Z Encyclopedia of Garden Plants, edited by
Christopher Brickell and Judy Zuk (London: DK Publishing, 1997)

Two Web Sites for Botanical Book Browsing

www.timberpress.com

www.kewbooks.com

One Web Site for the Study of Journalism

www.poynteronline.org

One Perfect Companion to Cultivating Words

Will Write for Food, by Dianne Jacob (New York: Marlowe and Company, 2005)

If you are interested in building a career in freelance writing, buy this helpful book! Yes, she is talking about food writing, but food writing is a kissing cousin to the subject at hand.

Six Books on Writing

Inventing the Truth: The Art and Craft of the Memoir, by William Zinsser (New York: Houghton Mifflin, 1995)

Lonely Planet Guide to Travel Writing, by Don George (Oakland: Lonely Planet Publications, 2005)

On Writing Well: An Informal Guide to Writing Nonfiction, by William Zinsser, 25th Anniversary Edition (New York: HarperCollins, 2001)

The Art of the Personal Essay, Phillip Lopate, ed. (New York: Random House, 1997)

The Situation and the Story: The Art of the Personal Narrative, by Vivian Gornick (New York: Farrar, Straus and Giroux, 2001)

Wild Mind: Living the Writer's Life, by Natalie Goldberg (New York: Bantam Books, 1990)

Two Books All Writers Should Have

Bryson's Dictionary of Troublesome Words: A Writer's Guide to Getting It Right, by Bill Bryson (New York: Broadway Books, 2002)

The Elements of Style, 4th edition, by William Strunk Jr. and E. B. White (Needham Heights, Mass: Allyn & Bacon, 2000, 1979)

Ten Books I Love

A Garlic Testament, by Stanley Crawford (New York: HarperPerennial, 1992)

African-American Gardens and Yards in the Rural South, by Richard Westmacott (Knoxville: The University of Tennessee Press, 1992)

American Garden Writing, Bonnie Marranca, ed. (New York: Penguin Books, 1989)

My Garden [Book], by Jamaica Kincaid (New York: Farrar, Straus and Giroux, 1999)

Oranges, by John McPhee (New York: Farrar, Straus and Giroux, 1967)

The Orchid Thief, by Susan Orlean (New York: Ballantine Books, 1998)

The Rural Life, by Verlyn Klinkenborg (Boston: Back Bay Books, 2002)

The 3,000 Mile Garden, by Roger Phillips & Leslie Land (London: Pan Books, 1995)

The Writer in the Garden, Jane Garmey, ed. (New York: Algonquin Books, 1999)

Yard Full of Sun, by Scott Calhoun (Tucson: Rio Nuevo Publishers, 2005)

Three Books on Travel and Plants and Life

Among Flowers: A Walk in the Himalaya, by Jamaica Kincaid (Washington, D.C., National Geographic Directions, 2005)

French Dirt, by Richard Goodman (New York: Algonquin Books, 2002)

In the Land of Blue Poppies, by Frank Kingdon Ward (New York: The Modern Library, 2003)

Four Writers to Read for the Rest of Your Life

M. F. K. Fisher

John McPhee

Vita Sackville-West

Gary Snyder

To Join the Garden Writers Association

GWA
10210 Leatherleaf Court
Manassas, VA 20111
703-257-1032
info@gardenwriters.org
www.gardenwriters.org

Appendix 2

Permissions

Richard Jaynes excerpt, p. 131, *Kalmia: Mountain Laurel and Related Species.* Copyright © 1997 Timber Press, Inc. Reprinted by permission.

Diane Ackerman excerpt, first paragraph on p. 18, from *Cultivating Delight: A Natural History of My Garden* © 2001 by Diane Ackerman. Reprinted by permission of HarperCollins Publishers, Inc.

"Reap What You Sow," copyright © 2003 by Mark Adams. Reprinted with the kind permission of the author.

"Out of the West Come More Reliable, Cold-Hardy Hyssops," copyright © 2003 by Erica Browne Grivas. Reprinted with the kind permission of the author.

Excerpt from "On Jupiter Island, Storm Took Heavy Toll on Residents' Seclusion," by Felicity Barringer. Copyright © 2005 by The New York Times Co. Reprinted with permission.

"Turning Cactuses into Connecticut Yankees," by Paula Panich. Copyright © 2002 by The New York Times Co. Reprinted with permission.

Quote from Leslie Land appears in Roger Phillips & Leslie Land, *The 3,000 Mile Garden,* Pan Books Ltd. Copyright © Roger Phillips and Leslie Land, 1992, 1995. Reprinted with the kind permission of Leslie Land.

Excerpt from "A Perfect Madness of Plants" by Verlyn Klinkenborg, from the *New York Times Magazine.* Copyright © 1999 by The New York Times Co. Reprinted with permission.

Appendix 3

Acknowledgments of Previously Published Material

John Muir quotation appears in his book *My First Summer in the Sierra,* Houghton Mifflin, 1911; reprint Sierra Club Books, 1988.

Vita Sackville-West's quotation appears in her book *The Garden Book,* first published in Britain by Michael Joseph Ltd., 1968, copyright © Vita Sackville-West.

"To Plant a Tree, Shrub, or Perennial," copyright © 1999 by Eugene Lawrence. Originally published in DiRT: *A Garden Journal from the Connecticut River Valley,* spring 1999.

Quotation from Lawrence Durrell's essay "Landscape and Character" appears in *The Lawrence Durrell Reader,* Carroll & Graf Publishers, copyright © 2004 by the Lawrence Durrell Estate.

Quotation from Maxine Hong Kingston, *The Fifth Book of Peace,* Alfred A. Knopf, copyright © 2003 Maxine Hong Kingston.

Natalie Goldberg's rule for writing appears in her book *Wild Mind: Living the Writer's Life.* Copyright © Bantam Books, 1990.

About the Author

PAULA PANICH, a journalist and garden writing instructor and coach, has been writing about plants and gardens for two decades. She holds a master of fine arts degree in creative writing from Warren Wilson College and teaches at the New York Botanical Garden and at the Huntington Library, Art Collections, and Botanical Gardens (San Marino, California), among other horticultural venues, and at Boston University. Her work has appeared in the *New York Times,* the *Washington Post, Gastronomica, Better Homes and Gardens,* and other publications. She is coauthor with Nora Burba Trulsson of *The Desert Southwest* and *Desert Southwest Gardens* (Bantam Books) and edits www.dirtagardenjournal.com. She divides her gardening and life between USDA Zones 5 (Northampton, Massachusetts) and 9 (Los Angeles). She thinks she has the best job in the world.